A SUMMARY OF

THE BEL

MUḤ MMAD

ﷺ

an English translation of

أنموذج اللبيب في خصائص الحبيب ﷺ

al-Khaṣā'iṣ aṣ-Ṣughrā

Anmūdhaj al-Labīb fī Khaṣā'iṣ al-Ḥabīb ﷺ

Imām Jalāluddīn as-Suyūṭī
(849AH/1445CE – 911AH/1505CE)

Translated by
Ṭāhir Maḥmood Kiānī

Ta-Ha Publishers Ltd.

First Published in June 2016

Published by:
Ta-Ha Publishers Ltd,
Unit 4, The Windsor Centre,
Windsor Grove, West Norwood,
London, SE27 9NT
UK

Website: www.tahapublishers.com
E-mail: support@tahapublishers.com

Original Arabic text by: Imām Jalāluddīn as-Suyūṭī
Translated by: Ṭāhir Maḥmood Kiānī
Cover and Book Design by: Shakir Abdulcadir .: opensquares.uk

A catalogue record of this book is available from the British Library
ISBN-13: 978-1-84200-161-5

Printed and bound by Mega Printed in Turkey

Dedication

For my uncles and my saintly aunt
(d. 19th Muḥarram 1437AH/1st November 2015CE)

Allāh سبحانه وتعالى bless them the best of the next world,
and joy and prosperity to those they leave behind.
Āmīn

بسم الله الرحمن الرحيم

Contents

PART 1

CHAPTER 1
*On what the Beloved Prophet Muhammad ﷺ
is personally specified with in this world.*   2

PART 2

⊗∿⊗

CHAPTER 1

On what the Beloved Prophet Muhammad ﷺ is specified with regarding obligations. The wisdom behind it is an increase in proximity and degrees. 44

CHAPTER 2

On what the Beloved Prophet Muhammad ﷺ is specified with regarding proscriptions. 50

CHAPTER 3

On what the Beloved Prophet Muhammad ﷺ is specified with regarding the lawful. 56

CHAPTER 4

On what the Beloved Prophet Muhammad ﷺ is specified with regarding honours and merits. 65

Concluding Salutations by the Translator 101

Bibliography 102

About the Translator 103

About the Author

Imām Abu'l-Faḍl 'Abdurraḥmān ibn Abū Bakr Jalāluddīn as-Suyūṭī (Allāh ﷻ have mercy on him) was born in the year 849AH/1445CE to non-Arab parents in the town of Suyūṭ (al-Asyūṭ), on the banks of the River Nile, almost 250 miles south of Cairo, Egypt.

His father, Kamāluddīn Abū Bakr (Allāh ﷻ have mercy on him) died in the year 855AH/1451CE, when Imām Jalāluddīn as-Suyūṭī was yet a child of six years, and thus, he was raised an orphan. His father had entrusted the Imām to, among others, the Ḥanafī master, Kamāluddīn ibn al-Humām (d. 861AH/1457CE), who took care of him.

His Teachers

Imām Jalāluddīn as-Suyūṭī had memorised the Holy Qur'ān when he was of the tender age of eight years. Thereafter, he pursued studies in Arabic language and grammar as well as all the Islāmic sciences, seeking knowledge from over a hundred and fifty teachers, who were all erudite scholars in their own right. Some of his illustrious teachers include: Sharafuddīn al-Munāwī, Sirājuddīn al-Bulqīnī, Aḥmad ibn Ibrāhīm ibn Naṣrullāh al-Kinānī al-Ḥanbalī, Aḥmad ibn Muḥammad al-Bulqīnī, Jalāluddīn al-Maḥallī, Shamsuddīn as-Sakhāwī, Sayfuddīn Qāsim ibn Qaṭlubaghā, etc. Allāh ﷻ have mercy on all of them. Āmīn.

His Students

There are numerous fortunate students who sought knowledge and wisdom from Imām Jalāluddīn as-Suyūṭī. The more famous of those students include:

Shamsuddīn ad-Dāwūdī al-Mālikī', Abdulwahhāb ash-Sha'rānī' and Muḥammad ibn Iyās, etc. Allāh ﷻ have mercy on all of them. Āmīn.

His Works

Imām Jalāluddīn as-Suyūṭī authored many scholarly treatises and beneficial works – over seven hundred – in all fields of knowledge, particularly in Qur'ānic sciences, history and Prophetic traditions (ḥadīths). Some of his famous works include: *Sharḥ al-Isti'ādhah wa'l-Basmalah, al-Jāmi' aṣ-Ṣaghīr, al-Jāmi' al-Kabīr, Tafsīr al-Jalālayn, Jam' al-Jawāmi', Tadrīb ar-Rāwī, al-Itqān fī 'Ulūm al-Qur'ān, Ta'rīkh al-Khulafā', al-Khaṣā'iṣ al-Kubrā, al-Khaṣā'is aṣ-Ṣughrā (Anmūdhaj al-Labīb fī Khaṣā'iṣ al-Ḥabīb* ﷺ*), al-Ḥāwī li'l-Fatāwī, Asrār Tartīb al-Qur'ān, Masālik al-Ḥunafā' fī Wāliday al-Muṣṭafā* ﷺ*, Sharḥ aṣ-Ṣudūr, Ikhtilāf al-Madhāhib, ad-Durr al-Manthūr, aṭ-Ṭibb an-Nabawī, Alfiyyat al-Ḥadīth, Ḥasan al-Maqṣid fī 'Amal al-Mawlid*, etc.

Among his works on the wonderful merits and qualities of the Prophet Muḥammad ﷺ, he authored *Kifāyat aṭ-Ṭālib al-Labīb fī Khaṣā'ṣ al-Ḥabīb* ﷺ (also known as *al-Khaṣā'iṣ al-Kubrā*) and its shorter version *Anmūdhaj al-Labīb fī Khaṣā'iṣ al-Ḥabīb* ﷺ (also known as *al-Khaṣā'iṣ aṣ-Ṣughrā*).

His Travels

His travels include those made to the Ḥijāz, Yemen, Damascus, Morocco, and Egypt, etc.

He assumed solitude for a period of twenty-two years (between the age of forty, until his death at the age of sixty-two years), dedicating the remainder of his life to writing, and that is the period wherein he is said to have authored most of his works.

His Affiliations

In Islāmic law, he was affiliated to the Shāfi'ī school of jurisprudence and legal methodology, and he had pledged his allegiance to the Shādhilī path in his spiritual affiliation. (*Tashyīd al-Ḥaqīqat al-'Aliyyah*)

His credal affiliation is linked to the Ash'arī school. (*Masālik al-Ḥunafā' fī Waliday al-Muṣṭafā* ﷺ)

Prophetic Vision

It is said, with reference to ash-Sha'rānī (898AH/1492CE – 973AH/1565CE) and an-Nabhānī (1265AH/1849CE – 1350AH/1932CE), that Imām Jalāluddīn as-Suyūṭī saw the Beloved Messenger Muḥammad ﷺ more than seventy times in the state of wakefulness, and he acquired knowledge directly from him ﷺ.

His Lofty Status

Imām Jalāluddīn as-Suyūṭī is well known throughout the world, due to his attractive style of writing and his appealing authorship.

He enjoyed a lofty status as a historian, a philologist, a ḥadīth expert, an exegete, an expert jurist, and moreover, a lover of Allāh ﷻ and His Beloved Messenger, Muḥammad ﷺ.

His Death

Imām Jalāluddīn as-Suyūṭī passed to the Next World on Thursday 18th Jumādā al-Ūlā 911AH/17th October 1505CE, after suffering an illness for seven days. He is buried in Ḥawsh Qawsūn in Cairo, Egypt.

It is said that his funeral prayer was also performed in absentia, as per its legality in the Shāfi'ī school, at the Umawī Masjid in Damascus, Syria.

This Book

Imām Jalāluddīn as-Suyūṭī originally gave this book the title *Anmūdhaj al-Labīb fī Khaṣā'iṣ al-Ḥabīb* ﷺ *– A Model for the Wise on the Unique Particulars of the Beloved* ﷺ, but it is better known as *al-Khaṣā'iṣ aṣ-Ṣughrā – A Summary of the Unique Particulars (of the Beloved Prophet Muḥammad* ﷺ*)*. The author himself states in its preface that he rendered this book a summary of the larger *Kifāyat aṭ-Ṭālib al-Labīb fī Khaṣāi'ṣ al-Ḥabīb – Sufficiency for the Wise Seeker of the Unique Particulars of the Beloved* ﷺ, better known as *al-Khaṣā'iṣ al-Kubrā – The Major Prophetic Particulars (on the Miracles of the Best of Creations* ﷺ*)*.

This Translation

Our translation of this wonderful masterpiece by Imām Jalāluddīn as-Suyūṭī commenced on 1st Muḥarram 1437AH/15th October 2015CE, and it concluded on 12th Rabīʿ al-Awwal 1437AH/24th December 2015CE.

For the source text, we used the online copy that is available at http://ansaralmostafa.mam9.com/t249-topic (accessed on 10th October 2015CE). We also referred to an Urdu translation, though that was mostly but not always consistent with the source text – in language, references or content structure and arrangement.

We have provided references to some of the ḥadīths mentioned herein for the benefit of the reader. As additions to the original text, we have also placed brief explanations as a continuation to it and as essential wording in square brackets so as to facilitate the reader in understanding the objective of the author. However, the text itself is such that where ambiguities and confusions may occur, though we have attempted to remove them all, the reader ought to refer to a qualified scholar or relevant texts. An example of such confusions is where the author has mentioned the legal permissibility for the Community of the Messenger of Allāh ﷺ joining two prayers when travelling, ill or when it is raining. This might seem a little odd to those who follow the Ḥanafī school, however, the author adhered to the Shāfiʿī school which permits it.

There are other suchlike legal as well as esoteric issues that one might not be comfortable in embracing at first, and thus it is important to refer to those of higher authority and detail for their explanation.

It is very noticeable that the text is not consistent, and it ebbs and flows at times. One may often find points mentioned in one section more appropriate to another section. Moreover, the source text lacks headings that might have provided the reader more clarity and understanding of each section. It is thus that we have inserted headings in square brackets to remedy such inconsistencies, render it flowing and remove its ebbing, and making clear the points that seem to be mentioned out of place in the source text without compromising its original arrangement and order.

Moreover, we have refrained from adding prayers of mercy and blessings to the names of the scholars cited herein, and hence, we make prior supplications for them to the Almighty that He عزّ وجلّ blesses their efforts, showers incessant divine mercy over their souls, and most importantly, accepts their love for the Beloved ﷺ. Āmīn.

Since we are prone to mistakes and forgetfulness, we would only be pleased if any mistakes herein were pointed out to us so that we may rectify them. However, any mistakes there may be are mine, and the good herein is from the mercy of Allāh ﷻ.

Our Gratitude and Prayers

We pray that Allāh ﷻ continues to bless the blessed name of Imām Jalāluddīn as-Suyūṭī – Allāh ﷻ shower His ﷻ mercy over him, for the invaluable treasure of knowledge and wisdom that he has left for us. Āmīn.

We would like to extend our gratitude to Dr. Abia Afsar-Siddiqui for her encouraging efforts in proofreading this text and editing it. May Allāh ﷻ shower His ﷻ divine mercy on her and her family. Āmīn.

We pray that Allāh ﷻ accepts the encouragement of my noble wife – my 'Rock', and her tolerating my 'spare time' being not so spare, as it is mostly spent inside books and at the computer. We also pray that He ﷻ bless my children – Zayn, Qudsia and Mahdia – with the true love of the Messenger of Allāh ﷺ and adopting the lifestyle that pleases him ﷺ.

We ask Allāh ﷻ to accept this humble effort of ours, and cause it to be a means of forgiveness for our sins, by the grace of His ﷻ Beloved Messenger Muḥammad ﷺ – on whom we invoke blessings and salutations for ever and ever.

Author's Preface

All praise is to Allāh ﷻ Who ﷻ perfected all things with His ﷻ wisdom and composed them well; sent His ﷻ Beloved Muḥammad ﷺ and cast light through him ﷺ into all the layers of pitch darkness; bestowed upon him ﷺ such miracles and unique particulars that no Prophet ﷺ or angel was bestowed; and rendered the angels his ﷺ army – who travel with him ﷺ wherever he ﷺ goes.

May Allāh ﷻ bless him ﷺ and grant him peace, his ﷺ Progeny ﷺ and his ﷺ Companions ﷺ – as long as ships continue to sail and the celestial sphere continues to revolve.

This is a fine specimen and a noble topic that I have summarised from my larger book[1] in which I have collected the Prophetic miracles and unique Prophetic particulars, together with their evidences, wherein I have sought ḥadīths that have been mentioned in relation to the station of prophethood and the greatness of its merits.

I have confined it to mentioning the unique [Prophetic] particulars in a succinct rendition, and I have distinguished herein each of its types separately. I have entitled it:

أَنْمُوْذَجُ اللَّبِيْبِ فِي خَصَائِصِ الْحَبِيْبِ

ﷺ

Anmūdhaj al-Labīb fī Khaṣā'iṣ al-Ḥabīb ﷺ

A Model for the Wise on the Unique Particulars of the Beloved ﷺ.

1 *Al-Khaṣā'iṣ al-Kubrā fī Mu'jizāt Khayr al-Warā* ﷺ – The Major Prophetic Particulars on the Miracles of the Best of Creations ﷺ, or *Kifāyat aṭ-Ṭālib al-Labīb fī Khaṣā'iṣ al-Ḥabīb* – Sufficiency for the Wise Seeker of the Unique Particulars of the Beloved ﷺ.

I have no ability except through Allāh ﷻ upon Whom ﷻ I rely and to Whom ﷻ I turn.

This book consists of two parts.

[Part 1 – On the unique particulars the Beloved Prophet Muḥammad ﷺ is specified with among all the Prophets ﷺ, and no Prophet ﷺ was given them prior to him ﷺ.

Part 2 – On the unique particulars the Beloved Prophet Muḥammad ﷺ is specified with from his ﷺ Community, some of which the Prophets ﷺ are known to share with him ﷺ, and some of which are not known.]

PART 1

On the unique particulars the Beloved Prophet Muḥammad ﷺ is specified with among all the Prophets ﷺ, and no Prophet ﷺ was given them prior to him ﷺ.

It has four chapters.

» [Chapter 1: On what the Beloved Prophet Muḥammad ﷺ is personally specified with in this world.

» Chapter 2: On what the Beloved Prophet Muḥammad ﷺ is specified with regarding his ﷺ Sacred Law for his ﷺ Community in this world.

» Chapter 3: On what the Beloved Prophet Muḥammad ﷺ is personally specified with in the Hereafter.

» Chapter 4: On what the Beloved Prophet Muḥammad ﷺ is specified with regarding his ﷺ Community in the Hereafter.]

CHAPTER

1

On what the Beloved Prophet Muḥammad ﷺ is personally specified with in this world.

[Prophet Muḥammad ﷺ]

He ﷺ is specified in that:

- he ﷺ is the first of the Prophets عليهم السلام to be created
- in the advancement of his ﷺ prophethood as he ﷺ was a Prophet when Prophet Ādam عليه السلام was intermingled as water and clay
- in the advancement of the oath being administered to him ﷺ
- he ﷺ was the first to proclaim "Of course!" on the day [when Allāh تعالى asked]:

أَلَسْتُ بِرَبِّكُمْ ۖ

Am I not your Lord?[2]

- Prophet Ādam عليه السلام and all creatures were created because of him ﷺ
- his ﷺ noble name being written on the Divine Throne (*'Arsh*); upon each heaven and whatever they contain, as well as the [various degrees of] Paradise and all the dominions
- the angels mentioning him ﷺ at every moment
- his ﷺ name being mentioned in the *adhān* (Call to Ritual Prayer) during the time of Prophet Ādam عليه السلام – and in the upper realms
- the administering of oath to the Prophets عليهم السلام – Prophet Ādam عليه السلام and to those after him عليهم السلام, that they عليهم السلام would believe in him ﷺ and assist him ﷺ
- the glad tidings of his ﷺ advent in the previous divine scriptures
- his ﷺ praise mentioned in them, [as well as] the praise of his ﷺ Companions رضي الله عنهم, his ﷺ Caliphs رضي الله عنهم and his ﷺ Community
- Iblīs barred from the heavens at his ﷺ birth
- the splitting of his ﷺ chest – according to one of two sayings, and that is the most correct
- the Seal of Prophethood stamped in his ﷺ back – level with his ﷺ heart, wherefrom Shayṭān would [otherwise] enter – the Seals [of Prophethood] of other Prophets عليهم السلام were on their right sides.

[His ﷺ Names]

[Furthermore, he ﷺ is specified in that:]

- he ﷺ has a thousand names

2. Holy Qur'ān, Sūrat al-A'rāf (7), Verse 172.

» his ﷺ name is derived from the [holy] Name of Allāh ﷻ
» he ﷺ was given approximately seventy names from the Names of Allāh ﷻ
» he ﷺ was named Aḥmad, and no one was given that name before him ﷺ.

These [aforementioned] unique particulars have been enumerated in a ḥadīth of [Ṣaḥīḥ] Muslim.

[Angels ﷷ]

[Furthermore:]

» the angels shading him ﷺ during his ﷺ journey
» his ﷺ being the most intellectually preponderant
» his ﷺ being bestowed with absolute beauty whereas Prophet Yūsuf ﷷ was given but a portion from it
» his ﷺ being embraced thrice at the beginning of the Revelation
» his ﷺ seeing [the Archangel] Jibrīl ﷷ in the form he ﷷ was created in.

Al-Bayhaqī has enumerated these [aforementioned].

[Some of His ﷺ Particulars]

[Furthermore, he ﷺ is specified with:]

» the cessation of soothsaying by virtue of his ﷺ being sent
» the custodianship of the heavens from eavesdropping [by devils] and [their] being pelted with meteors.

Ibn Sab' has enumerated these [aforementioned].

[Furthermore:]

» the resurrection of his ﷺ parents that they may declare belief in him ﷺ
» his ﷺ being promised protection from people.

[His ﷺ Night Journey and Heavenly Ascension]

[Furthermore:]

» his ﷺ being taken on the Night Journey (*Isrā'*), and whatever he ﷺ was bestowed with [including] permeance through the seven heavens and the highest station and reaching the station of 'The Meeting of the Two Bows' (*Qāba Qawsayn*)
» his ﷺ treading where no divinely-sent Prophet ﷷ had trod and nor any proximate angel ﷷ

» the Prophets ﷺ made to rise from the graves for him ﷺ, and his ﷺ leading the prayer with them ﷺ and with the angels
» his ﷺ touring Paradise and the Fire [of Hell].

Al-Bayhaqī has enumerated these [aforementioned].

[Furthermore:]
» his ﷺ beholding the major signs of his ﷺ Lord ﷻ
» his ﷺ beholding Him ﷻ until:

مَا زَاغَ ٱلْبَصَرُ وَمَا طَغَىٰ

The vision did not sway and nor did it overtake[3]

» his ﷺ seeing the Most High Maker ﷻ twice
» his ﷺ mounting the Burāq – according to one of two sayings.

[Angels Assisting Him ﷺ]

[Furthermore:]
» the angels fighting alongside him ﷺ
» their travelling with him ﷺ wherever he ﷺ would go – travelling behind him ﷺ.

[His ﷺ Book]

[Furthermore:]
» his ﷺ being given the Book, though he ﷺ was not taught by any created being – neither reading and nor writing
» his ﷺ Book is miraculous and safeguarded from any alteration or distortion over the passing of epochs.

[It:]
» comprises of whatever all the [previous] scriptures comprised of and more
» is comprehensive of all things
» is independent of all else
» is simplified to memorise
» was revealed piecemeal

3. Holy Qur'ān, Sūrat an-Najm (53), Verse 17.

» is in seven modes [of recitation]
» is in seven chapters
» is in every language.
Ibn an-Naqīb has enumerated these [aforementioned].

[Furthermore:]
» recitation of each of its letters is ten rewards.
Az-Zarkashī has enumerated this.

The author of *at-Taḥrīr* said: "The Qur'ān is made superior to all the [divinely-] revealed books with thirty qualities that the others do not have."

In *al-Minhāj*, al-Ḥalīmī said: "It is of the great status of the Qur'ān that Allāh ﷻ has made it specific – that it is an invitation as well as a proof; never was this for any Prophet ﷺ before. Previous Prophets ﷺ were given an invitation and thereafter a separate proof, whereas Allāh ﷻ has combined them both in the Qur'ān for His Messenger [Muḥammad] ﷺ – it is thus an invitation by its meanings; a proof in its words. It is sufficient an honour for an invitation that its proof be with it, and it is sufficient an honour for a proof that its invitation not be detached from it."

[Furthermore:]
» he ﷺ was bestowed from the treasures of the Divine Throne when no-one else was given therefrom
» he ﷺ was specified with the *Basmalah*, the Fātiḥah, the Āyat al-Kursī, the Ending of Sūrat al-Baqarah[4], the *as-Sab' aṭ-Ṭiwāl*[5], and the *Mufaṣṣal* (Distinct) [Sūrahs of the Qur'ān]
» his ﷺ miracle continues until the Day of Judgement – it is the Qur'ān, whereas the miracles of all the Prophets ﷺ ceased to exist after their times.

4.
رَبَّنَا لَا تُؤَاخِذْنَآ إِن نَّسِينَآ أَوْ أَخْطَأْنَاۚ رَبَّنَا وَلَا تَحْمِلْ عَلَيْنَآ إِصْرًا كَمَا حَمَلْتَهُۥ عَلَى ٱلَّذِينَ مِن قَبْلِنَاۚ رَبَّنَا وَلَا تُحَمِّلْنَا مَا لَا طَاقَةَ لَنَا بِهِۦۖ وَٱعْفُ عَنَّا وَٱغْفِرْ لَنَا وَٱرْحَمْنَآۚ أَنتَ مَوْلَىٰنَا فَٱنصُرْنَا عَلَى ٱلْقَوْمِ ٱلْكَٰفِرِينَ (٢:٢٨٦)

Holy Qur'ān, Sūrat al-Baqarah (2), Verse 286.

5. The *as-Sab' aṭ-Ṭiwāl* (Long Seven *Sūrahs*) are: 1. al-Baqarah (2), 2. Āl 'Imrān (3), 3. an-Nisā' (4), 4. al-Mā'idah (5), 5. al-An'ām (6), 6. al-A'rāf (7) and 7. al-Anfāl (8) + at-Tawbah (9) together, or Yūnus (10). (Al-Bayhaqī, *Shu'ab al-Īmān*, Chapter *Dhikr as-Sab' aṭ-Ṭuwāl*, Ḥadīths 2417 – 2419) – see *al-Fawz al-Kabīr – The Greatest Victory*, Ta-Ha Publishers Ltd., 2014, page 136, footnote 508.

[His ﷺ Miracles]

[Furthermore:]

» he ﷺ has more miracles than all the Prophets ﷺ – it is said: "They reach a thousand," and it is said: "Three thousand," other than the Qur'ān – it itself contains approximately sixty thousand miracles[6].

Al-Ḥalīmī said: "Besides the sheer number of miracles, there are other qualities within them, and that is their not being among the miracles of others, such as forming material objects, as it is among the miracles specific to our Prophet [Muḥammad] ﷺ."

[Furthermore:]

» all the miracles and qualities that the previous Prophets ﷺ were bestowed with were gathered together for him ﷺ, whereas they were not gathered together for anyone else, but rather, each one ﷺ was specified with one type.

[Furthermore:]

» he ﷺ was given [the miracles of] the Splitting of the Moon, the [Greeting of] Salutation by the Stones, the Crying of the Date-Palm Trunk, the Flowing of Water from between His ﷺ Fingers – nothing the like of these was established for any of the [other] Prophets ﷺ.

Ibn 'Abdussalām has mentioned these.

[Furthermore:]

» some have said: "Allāh ﷻ has specified some [of the Prophets] ﷺ with miracles in acts – such as Prophet Mūsā ﷺ; some in qualities – such as Prophet 'Īsā ﷺ; and our Prophet [Muḥammad] ﷺ with a combination [of both] – in order to render him ﷺ distinct
» the trees speaking and bearing witness to him ﷺ in prophethood, and their answering to his ﷺ call
» resurrecting the dead and speaking to them
» suckling infants speaking [to him ﷺ], and bearing witness to his ﷺ prophethood."

Al-Badr ad-Damāmīnī[7] has mentioned these.

---

6. The Qur'ān's miracles number seventy thousand. (*Al-Khaṣā'iṣ aṣ-Ṣughrā* (Urdu), translated by 'Allāmah 'Abdurrasūl Arshad, Zia-ul-Qur'an Publications, Lahore, Pakistan, Rabī' al-Awwal 1406AH).
7. He is Badruddīn ad-Damāmīnī (763AH/1362CE – 828AH/1425CE).

[His ﷺ Being the Seal of Prophethood]

[It is from among his ﷺ unique particulars that:]

» he ﷺ is the Seal of the Prophets عليهم السلام

» [he ﷺ is] the last of them عليهم السلام to be sent, and thus, there is no prophet after him ﷺ

» his ﷺ Law shall continue unabrogated until the Day of Judgement; it abrogates all the Laws prior to it

» if the Prophets عليهم السلام witness him ﷺ, following him ﷺ would be obliged upon them عليهم السلام

» his ﷺ Book and his ﷺ Law contain the abrogating and the abrogated

» his ﷺ invitation [to the Truth] is inclusively generic for all the people

» he ﷺ has more followers than any of the Prophets عليهم السلام.

[His ﷺ Being the Comprehensive Prophet]

[Furthermore:]

» as-Subkī said: "He ﷺ was sent comprehensively to all creatures since [the time of] Prophet Ādam عليه السلام

» the Prophets عليهم السلام are his ﷺ representatives, sent with Laws concerned with him ﷺ and thus he ﷺ is the Prophet ﷺ of the Prophets عليهم السلام

» he ﷺ was sent to the jinn – according to [scholarly] consensus, and to the angels – according to one of two sayings." As-Subkī has preferred this [saying].

» Al-Bārizī said: "And [he ﷺ was sent] to the animals, inorganic bodies, stones and trees."

[Allāh سبحانه وتعالى] sent him ﷺ as a Mercy to all the Worlds – even to the disbelievers, by delaying the punishment [to them] and their not being punished promptly as used to happen to previous rejecting nations

» that Allāh سبحانه وتعالى has sworn by his ﷺ life

» He سبحانه وتعالى has sworn by his ﷺ messengership

» He سبحانه وتعالى has undertaken to refute his ﷺ enemies Himself سبحانه وتعالى.

[Allāh ﷻ Addressing Him ﷺ]

[It is from among his ﷺ unique particulars that:]

» Allāh ﷻ has addressed him ﷺ in terms gentler than those in which He ﷻ has addressed [other] Prophets ﷩

» in His ﷻ Book, He ﷻ has attached his ﷺ name to His ﷻ Own Name

» upon the world has He ﷻ obliged to him ﷺ complete and unconditional obedience and support, without any exception

» He ﷻ has described him ﷺ in His ﷻ Book, limb by limb

» He ﷻ has not addressed him ﷺ in the Qur'ān by his ﷺ name, but rather:

يَٰٓأَيُّهَا ٱلنَّبِيُّ

O Prophet[8]

يَٰٓأَيُّهَا ٱلرَّسُولُ

O Messenger[9]

» He ﷻ has proscribed the Community from calling to him ﷺ by his ﷺ name.

[Furthermore:]

» [Imām] ash-Shāfi'ī has detested it for us to call him ﷺ: '*Rasūl* (Messenger),' but rather [we should call him ﷺ], '*Rasūlu'Llāh* (Messenger of Allāh) ﷺ,' because the former lacks the respect there is in the ascription [i.e. the latter].

[Honouring Him ﷺ]

[Furthermore:]

» Allāh ﷻ has obligated upon anyone who converses with him ﷺ in secrecy to give in charity prior to conversing with him ﷺ in secrecy, [but] then it was abrogated

» Allāh ﷻ has not shown him ﷺ anything of his ﷺ Community that would cause him ﷺ discomfort, until He ﷻ took his ﷺ life, as opposed to all the Prophets ﷩

» he ﷺ is '*Ḥabīburraḥmān* (Beloved of the Divinely-Compassionate)'.

8. Holy Qur'ān, Sūrat al-Aḥẓāb (33), Verse 45.
9. Holy Qur'ān, Sūrat al-Mā'idah (5), Verse 41.

[On What was Combined for Him ﷺ]

[Furthermore:]

» love and intimacy were combined for him ﷺ; as well as conversing and beholding

» Allāh ﷻ conversed with him ﷺ at the Lote-Tree of the Final Station (*Sidrat al-Muntahā*), whereas He ﷻ conversed with Prophet Mūsā ﷺ at the Mountain.

Ibn 'Abdussalām has enumerated these [aforementioned].

[Furthermore:]

» the Two Directions for Prayer (*Qiblah*) – Makkah and Bayt al-Maqdis – were combined for him ﷺ

» as were the Two Migrations – Bayt al-Maqdis and Madīnah

» ruling over the Outward and the Inward were combined for him ﷺ

» the Sacred Law (*Sharī'ah*) and the Divine Reality (*Ḥaqīqah*) were combined for him ﷺ

» the Prophets ﷺ only have one of the two [aforementioned], for which the evidence is the story of Prophet Mūsā ﷺ with Khaḍir ﷺ, and his ﷺ saying [to the other]: "I have certain knowledge that you must learn, and you have certain knowledge that I must learn."

[On What He ﷺ was Bestowed]

[It is from among his ﷺ unique particulars that:]

» he ﷺ was assisted with awe to the distance of a month [in travelling time] in front of him ﷺ and a month [in travelling time] behind him ﷺ

» he ﷺ was given comprehensive speech (*jawāmi' al-kalim*)

» he ﷺ was given the keys to the treasures of the earth upon a piebald horse covered with an amaranth of sarcenet

» Allāh ﷻ spoke to him ﷺ in all the various form of Revelation.

Ibn 'Abdussalām has enumerated these [aforementioned].

[Furthermore:]

» [the Angel] Isrāfīl ﷺ descended to him ﷺ, and he ﷺ has never descended to any Prophet ﷺ prior to him ﷺ.

Ibn Sab' has enumerated these [aforementioned].

[Furthermore:]
» prophethood and [political] authority were combined for him ﷺ.
Al-Ghazālī has mentioned this in *al-Iḥyā'*.

He ﷺ was given knowledge of all things other than the five that are mentioned in Sūrah Luqmān[10], and they are, as Allāh ﷻ says:

إِنَّ ٱللَّهَ عِندَهُۥ عِلْمُ ٱلسَّاعَةِ وَيُنَزِّلُ ٱلْغَيْثَ وَيَعْلَمُ مَا فِى ٱلْأَرْحَامِ ۖ وَمَا تَدْرِى نَفْسٌ مَّاذَا تَكْسِبُ غَدًا ۖ وَمَا تَدْرِى نَفْسٌ بِأَىِّ أَرْضٍ تَمُوتُ

Verily, it is Allāh ﷻ with Whom is the knowledge of the Hour. He ﷻ sends down the rain, and knows what is in the wombs. No soul knows what it will earn tomorrow, and no soul knows in what land it will die.[11]

It is also said: "He ﷺ was given them but he ﷺ was encouraged to conceal them, and the difference lies regarding the soul also."

[Furthermore:]
» the matter regarding the Dajjāl (Antichrist) has been made clear to him ﷺ such that it was not made clear to anyone
» he ﷺ has been promised absolution while he ﷺ was walking, living and sound
» tribute to him ﷺ has been made high; Allāh ﷻ is not mentioned in the *adhān*, the *khuṭbah* (sermon) or the *tashahhud* (sitting posture in prayer) except that he ﷺ is mentioned with Him ﷻ.

[His ﷺ being Guaranteed Safety and Forgiveness]

Ibn 'Abbās ﷺ said: "Allāh ﷻ has not guaranteed safety to anyone among His ﷻ creatures except for Muḥammad ﷺ. He ﷻ has said:

لِيَغْفِرَ لَكَ ٱللَّهُ مَا تَقَدَّمَ مِن ذَنۢبِكَ وَمَا تَأَخَّرَ

... so that Allāh ﷻ forgives for you your past and future accusations[12]

and He ﷻ said to the angels:

10. Holy Qur'ān, Sūrah Luqmān (31).
11. Holy Qur'ān, Sūrah Luqmān (31), Verse 34.
12. Holy Qur'ān, Sūrat al-Fatḥ (48), Verse 2.

وَمَن يَقُلْ مِنْهُمْ إِنِّىٓ إِلَٰهٌ مِّن دُونِهِۦ فَذَٰلِكَ نَجْزِيهِ جَهَنَّمَ

And if any of them say, 'Verily, I am a god besides Him (i.e. Allāh),'
such a person We shall punish in Hell.[13]"

'Umar ibn al-Khaṭṭāb ※ said: "No soul knows as to what is to happen to it, but not this man ※ about whom ※ was made clear to us that his ※ past and future accusations have been forgiven for him ※."

It was related by al-Ḥākim.

[On What was Presented before Him ※]

His ※ entire Community was presented before him ※ and he ※ saw them, and he ※ was shown what was to happen to his ※ Community until the Last Hour comes.

Al-Isfarā'īnī said: "The creatures were presented to him ※ – all of them, from Prophet Ādam ※ and all those after him ※, just as Prophet Ādam ※ was given knowledge of all things."

» He ※ is the Leader of the descendants of Prophet Ādam ※
» the most noble to Allāh ※ of all creatures
» the most excellent of all the Messengers ※ [sent by Allāh ※] and of all the proximate angels. He ※ is more perspicacious than all of creation.

Ibn Surāqah has enumerated these [aforementioned].

[On His ※ Being Supported]

[Furthermore:]

» he ※ was supported by four ministers:
   1. Jibrīl ※
   2. Mīkā'īl ※
   3. Abū Bakr ※ and
   4. 'Umar ※
» he ※ was given fourteen nobles as his ※ Companions ※ whereas every [other] Prophet ※ was given seven
» one who seeks his ※ company is in safety
» his ※ wives were his ※ aides.

---

13. Holy Qur'ān, Sūrat al-Anbiyā' (21), Verse 29.

[The Superiority of What is Ascribed to Him ﷺ]

[It is from among his ﷺ unique particulars that:]

» his ﷺ daughters and his ﷺ wives are the most excellent women from all creation

» the reward of and admonishment to his ﷺ wives is multiplied

» his ﷺ Companions ؓ are the best of all creation other than the Prophets ؑ; they ؓ approximate the number of the Prophets ؑ; they ؓ are all distinguished jurists (*mujtahid*), and thus, the Holy Prophet ﷺ said:

أَصْحَابِيْ كَالنُّجُوْمِ بِأَيِّهِمْ اِقْتَدَيْتُمْ اِهْتَدَيْتُمْ

My Companions are like the stars; any of them you follow, you shall be guided

» his ﷺ masjid is the most excellent of masjids.

[His ﷺ City]

[It is from among his ﷺ unique particulars that:]

» his ﷺ city is, by consensus, the most excellent of cities, other than Makkah – according to one of two sayings, but this is the most preferred opinion.

» Al-Māwardī and al-Qāḍī 'Iyāḍ said: "The snakes of the City of the Prophet ﷺ (Madīnah) are not to be killed without being warned. The ḥadīth related about snakes being warned is specific to Madīnah."

» Makkah was made lawful to him ﷺ for the portion of a day

» the area was consecrated [as a ḥaram] between the two lava fields of Madīnah

its earth is peace-giving

its dust cures leprosy

half the stomachs of its goats and sheep is equal to twice as that of the goats and sheep of other cities

» the Dajjāl cannot enter it, and nor plagues

» fever was transferred from it to al-Juḥfah the very first time it approached Madīnah. Thereafter, when Jibrīl ؑ brought the fever and the plague, the Prophet ﷺ halted the fever at Madīnah and he ﷺ dispatched the plague to ash-Shām (the Levant). Thereafter, and with the will of the Prophet ﷺ, when the fever returned to Madīnah it could not affect any of its residents until it came and stopped at his ﷺ door. It sought permission as to where he ﷺ would send it, and so he ﷺ dispatched it towards the Anṣār (the Helpers).

[His ﷺ Further Particulars]

[It is from among his ﷺ unique particulars that:]

» the dead in their graves are questioned about him ﷺ

» the Angel of Death sought his ﷺ permission, whereas it did not seek the permission of any Prophet عليه السلام prior to him ﷺ

» marriage to any of his ﷺ wives after him ﷺ is prohibited, as is having sexual relations with his bondmaid

» the piece of land wherein he ﷺ is buried is more excellent than the Ka'bah and also the Divine Throne

» it is prohibited [for anyone] to adopt his ﷺ filial appellation (*kunyah*); this is also said with regard to his ﷺ name 'Muḥammad' ﷺ; it is also said with regard to taking the name 'Qāsim' – so that one's father may not be given the filial appellation 'Abu'l-Qāsim'.

An-Nawawī has reported this in the *Commentary on Muslim.*

[Furthermore:]

» it is permitted for Allāh ﷻ to swear by him ﷺ, but not for anyone else.

Ibn 'Abdussalām has mentioned this.

[Furthermore:]

» his ﷺ private parts have never been seen, and had anyone seen them his eyes would have been expunged

» he ﷺ does not commit a mistake.

Ibn Abū Hurayrah and al-Māwardī have enumerated this.

» Some have said: "… and nor forgetfulness."

An-Nawawī has reported this in the *Commentary on Muslim.*

Al-Bārizī has stated in *Tawthīq 'Ura'l-Īmān:* "It is among his ﷺ unique particulars that he ﷺ is:

» an amalgamation of the qualities of all the Prophets عليهم السلام

» he ﷺ is the Prophet ﷺ of the Prophets عليهم السلام

» there is no Prophet عليه السلام who has a particularity of his عليه السلام prophethood [to undertake] in his عليه السلام respective Community except that one of the scholars in this Community represents that Prophet عليه السلام in his عليه السلام respective Community, and assumes that domain during his time. There is a ḥadīth narrated in this regard:

عُلَمَاءُ أُمَّتِيْ كَأَنْبِيَاءِ بَنِيْ إِسْرَائِيْلَ

The scholars of my Community are like the Prophets ﷺ of the Banū Isrā'īl.

And it has been narrated: 'A scholar among his people is like a Prophet ﷺ to his Community.'"

He said: "Among his ﷺ specific traits is that Allāh ﷻ has named him ﷺ 'Abdullāh – and He ﷻ has not applied this title to anyone but him ﷺ, but rather, [in reference to others,] He ﷻ said:

إِنَّهُۥ كَانَ عَبْدًا شَكُورًا

Verily, he was a grateful servant[14]

[with regards to Prophet Nūḥ ﷺ], and

نِعْمَ ٱلْعَبْدُ

How excellent a servant is he[15]

[with regards to Prophet Ayyūb ﷺ].

[Furthermore:]

» among his ﷺ specific traits is that there is no [mention of] blessings from Allāh ﷻ upon anyone other than him ﷺ in the Qur'ān or otherwise – it is a quality that Allāh ﷻ has specified him ﷺ with, exclusive to all the other Prophets ﷺ."

Ends [al-Bārizī's statement].

His ﷺ names are textual, as are the Names of Allāh ﷻ. This is verified in *Al-Arba'īn aṭ-Ṭā'iyyah.*

[Ends Chapter 1.]

14. Holy Qur'ān, Sūrat al-Isrā' (17), Verse 3.
15. Holy Qur'ān, Sūrah Ṣād (38), Verse 44.

CHAPTER

2

On what the Beloved Prophet Muḥammad ﷺ is specified with regarding his ﷺ Sacred Law for his ﷺ Community in this world.

[Unique Particulars for the Community of Prophet Muḥammad ﷺ]

[For his ﷺ Community] he ﷺ is specified with:

» the spoils [of war] being made lawful

» the entire earth being made a place for ritual prayer; previous nations could only pray in synagogues and churches

» the dust being made pure for *tayammum* (dry substitute ablution) – as an alternative to *wuḍū'* (ritual ablution) – according to one of two opinions, and this is more correct. Only previous Prophets ﷺ were permitted this but not their Communities.

There is a text related to Ibn Surāqah in *al-A'dād*:

» he ﷺ is specified with performing complete *wuḍū'*, *tayammum* and wiping the *khuffs*

» water is rendered a removing agent for filth

» filth does not affect a large body of water

» cleansing oneself [of impure excreta] with solids.

Abū Sa'īd an-Nīsābūrī has mentioned this in *Sharaf al-Muṣṭafā*, and Ibn Surāqah in *al-A'dād*. [And:]

» combining water and stone [in cleansing excreta].

[Ritual Prayers]

[Furthermore:]

» a combination of the five ritual prayers; they were not combined for anyone [before]

» they are an expiation for whatever [sin] takes place between them

» the *'ishā'* prayer; no-one prayed it [before]

» the *adhān* and the *iqāmah* (Call to the Commencement of Congregational Prayer)

» commencing the ritual prayer with the [consecratory] *takbīr* (*Allāhu Akbar*)

» saying '*āmīn*'

» bowing [in ritual prayer] – according to what a large group of [Qur'ānic] exegetes have stated

» and to say:

اَللّٰهُمَّ رَبَّنَا لَكَ الْحَمْدُ

Our Lord! To You is all praise

» the prohibition of talking during ritual prayer
» facing the Ka'bah [when praying]
» forming rows in ritual prayer like the rows of angels
» the congregation for ritual prayer

as understood by the statement of Ibn Farishtah in the *Commentary on al-Mujma'*.

[Furthermore:]

» greeting with salutations [by saying '*as-salāmu 'alaykum*'] – which is the greeting of the angels and the inhabitants of Paradise
» Friday being a day of festivity for him ﷺ and his ﷺ Community
» the moment of acceptance
» the 'Īd al-Aḍḥā.

Abū Sa'īd, in *Sharaf al-Muṣṭafā*, and Ibn Surāqah, have stated that:

» he ﷺ is specified with Friday's ritual prayer (*ṣalāt al-jumu'ah*)
» as well as congregational ritual prayer
» ritual prayer of the night (*ṣalāt al-layl*)
» ritual prayers of the two 'īds (*ṣalāt al-'īdayn*)
» ritual prayers of the two eclipses (*ṣalāt al-kusūf* – solar eclipse and *ṣalāt al-khusūf* – lunar eclipse)
» ritual prayer for seeking rain (*ṣalāt al-istisqā'*)
» the odd-numbered ritual prayer (*ṣalāt al-witr*).

Ends [statement].

[Furthermore:]

» curtailment of ritual prayer when travelling
» joining two prayers when travelling, when it is raining and when one is ill – according to one of two opinions, and this is the more preferred.[16]

[Furthermore:]

» the prayer in the state of fear (*ṣalāt al-khawf*); it was not legally permitted for anyone among the Communities prior to us
» the prayer during intense fear in the heat of battle, anywhere and facing any direction.

16. This not the case with the Ḥanafī school.

[The Month of Ramaḍān]

[Furthermore, he ﷺ is specified with:]

» the month of Ramaḍān.

Al-Qawnawī has mentioned this in the *Commentary on at-Taʿarruf*.

[Furthermore, during the month of Ramaḍān:]

» Shayṭāns are bound in it

» Paradise is decorated during it

» the malodour from the mouth of the one who is fasting is more pleasing to Allāh ﷻ than the scent of musk

» the angels seek forgiveness for them [i.e. those who are fasting] until they duly break their fast

» they [i.e. those who are fasting] are forgiven during the last of its nights

» the pre-dawn meal

» hastening the due breaking of fast

» permissibility of eating, drinking and sexual relations during the night until dawn; it was forbidden after sleep to do as such among those prior to us – as well as during the early days of Islām, but then it was abrogated

» prohibition of joining two fasts; it was permissible to those prior to us

» permissibility to speak during fasting; it was prohibited to those prior to us, as opposed to the ritual prayer.

Ibn al-ʿArabī has enumerated these [aforementioned] in *al-Aḥwadhī*.

[Furthermore:]

» the *Laylat al-Qadr* (Night of Power) – as an-Nawawī has mentioned in the *Commentary on al-Muhadhdhab*

» the rendering of the fasting on the Day of ʿArafah an expiation for two years, as it is his ﷺ sunnah (Prophetic practice)

» and the fasting on the Day of ʿĀshūrā' an expiation for one year, as it is the sunnah of Prophet Mūsā ﷺ

» the Day of ʿArafah [per sé].

Al-Qawnawī has mentioned these in the *Commentary on at-Taʿarruf*.

[More Particulars for His ﷺ Community]

[Furthermore, he ﷺ is specified with his ﷺ Community:]

» washing both hands after having food for two good deeds, as it is his ﷺ sunnah; for one good deed prior to him ﷺ as it is prescribed in the Tawrāh (Torah)

» bathing in a spring water, as it removes harms

» reciting:

إِنَّا لِلّٰهِ وَإِنَّآ إِلَيْهِ رَاجِعُونَ

Verily, we belong to Allāh ﷻ *and to Him* ﷻ *shall we return*[17]

and:

لَا حَولَ وَلَا قُوَّةَ إِلَّا بِاللهِ الْعَلِيِّ الْعَظِيْمِ

There is no strength or power except through Allāh ﷻ[18]

when suffering a calamity.

[Distinction from the People of the Scripture]

[Furthermore, the Community of Prophet Muḥammad ﷺ is specified with:]

» the niche of the grave; it was a trench for the People of the Scripture (*Ahl al-Kitāb*)

» slaughtering by stabbing the vein at the lower part of the neck (*naḥr*); for them [i.e. the People of the Scripture], it was [merely] slaughtering by cutting the four vessels (*dhabḥ*) – according to what Mujāhid and 'Ikrimah said.

[Furthermore, the Community of Prophet Muḥammad ﷺ is specified with:]

» parting the hair; they [i.e. the People of the Scripture] let it hang loose without gathering it together

» dying the hair; they would not alter grey and white hairs

» letting the beard grow and trimming the moustache; they would shorten the beard and let the moustache grow

» they would provide for the males and not the females, but it is prescribed for us to provide for both of them together.

---

17. Holy Qur'ān, Sūrat al-Baqarah (2), Verse 156.
18. Al-Bukhārī, *al-Jāmiʿ aṣ-Ṣaḥīḥ*; Muslim, *al-Musnad aṣ-Ṣaḥīḥ*; Abū Dāwūd, *as-Sunan*; etc.

[Furthermore, the Community of Prophet Muḥammad ﷺ is specified with:]

- not standing for the funeral
- hastening the *maghrib* and *fajr* [prayers]
- disapproval of wrapping the cloth around oneself in such a manner that no place remains whence one may project his hands
- disapproval of fasting on a Friday on its own; the Jews would fast on the day of their festivity on its own
- fasting on the ninth together with the tenth of Muḥarram
- prostrating on the forehead; they would prostrate on the edge [of the head]
- disapproval of swaying during ritual prayer; they would sway
- disapproval of closing the eyes during [ritual prayer]
- [disapproval of] standing with arms akimbo [during ritual prayer]
- [disapproval of] standing up to supplicate after it [i.e. ritual prayer]
- [disapproval of] the imām reciting from the written copy of the Qur'ān during it [i.e. ritual prayer]
- [disapproval of] occupying oneself with cords during it [i.e. ritual prayer].

[Furthermore, it is permitted for the Community of Prophet Muḥammad ﷺ:]

- to eat on the Day of 'Īd prior to ritual prayer; the People of the Scripture would not eat on the day of their festivity until after they had prayed
- to offer ritual prayer in shoes and slippers.[19]

It is reported by Ibn 'Umar ﷺ that when their imāms would recite, the Banū Isrā'īl would respond to them; but Allāh ﷻ has disapproved that for this Community. He ﷻ said:

وَإِذَا قُرِئَ ٱلْقُرْءَانُ فَٱسْتَمِعُواْ لَهُۥ وَأَنصِتُواْ

And when the Qur'ān is recited, listen to it attentively and pay heed…[20]

[It is stated] in *al-Mustadrak* that he ﷺ forbade a man who was sat resting on his left hand during ritual prayer. He ﷺ said: "It is the prayer of the Jews."

19. This is dependent on circumstances.
20. Holy Qur'ān, Sūrat al-A'rāf (7), Verse 204.

[Furthermore:]

- » our women are permitted to visit the masjids; the women of the Banū Isrā'īl were prohibited
- » their laws permitted abrogation of the ruling if the litigant raised the case with another judge who opposed the decision.

[Distinction in Attire]

[Furthermore:]

- » wearing of crests in turbans – they are the distinctions of angels
- » wearing sheets up to the midst of the lower legs
- » disapproval of allowing clothing to hang loose on either side (*sadl*) during ritual prayer, as well as the low-cut pallium
- » [disapproval of] tying the shirt at its middle
- » [disapproval of] cutting the hair in patches of varied lengths.

[Further Distinctions of His ﷺ Community]

[Furthermore:]

- » the lunar months
- » endowments
- » bequeathing a third when near death
- » hastening the funeral

[are all particulars of the Community of Prophet Muḥammad ﷺ].

[The Best Community]

[Furthermore, Prophet Muḥammad ﷺ is specified with:]

his ﷺ Community being:

- » the best community
- » the last community
- » they [i.e. the other communities] shall be outshone by it but it shall not be outshone
- » two names from the Names of Allāh ﷻ have been derived for it; *Muslim* (peacemaker) and *Mu'min* (giver of security)
- » their religion being named 'Islām'; this was the description of the [previous] Prophets ﷺ but not of their Communities.

'Abdullāh ibn Yazīd al-Anṣārī said: "You should adopt the names for yourselves that Allāh ﷻ has given you; Ḥanīfiyyah, Islām and Īmān."

[Special Permission for His ﷺ Community]

[Furthermore:]

» the burden that was upon previous Communities has been lifted away from them [i.e. the Muslims]
» hoarding wealth is permitted for them, provided they intend to pay *zakāh* (mandatory poor-due) from it
» much has been made lawful to them of what was made strict for those before them
» no objection has been placed against them in religious affairs.

[Furthermore:]

» it is permitted for them to eat the meat of camel, ostrich, onager, goose, duck, all kinds of fish, fats, and non-flowing blood – like liver, spleen and veins. [It is reported] in a ḥadīth:

أُحِلَّتْ لَنَا مَيْتَتَانِ وَدَمَانِ: السَّمَكُ وَالجَرَادُ، وَالكَبِدُ وَالطِّحَالُ

Two kinds of dead meats and two kinds of blood are lawful for us; fish and locust, and liver and spleen.[21]

[Furthermore:]

» being taken to task for making a mistake or forgetfulness has been removed from them, as well as that which they are coerced to do [as well as] intrapersonal thought.

[Furthermore:]

» if any one of them [i.e. the Muslims] thinks of committing a sin but does not do it, it is not recorded as a sin but a good deed – but if they do it, it is recorded as a single sin
» if any one of them thinks of doing a good deed but does not do it, it is recorded as one good deed – and if they do it, it is recorded as [somewhere] between tenfold and seven hundredfold.

21. Aḥmad, *al-Musnad*.

[Legal Concessions for His ﷺ Community]

[Furthermore:]

» killing them [i.e. the Muslims] as a means of repentance
» gouging out the eyes for looking at the unlawful
» cutting off the place [defiled with] impurity
» [paying] a quarter of wealth as *zakāh* (mandatory alms-giving)

[have been removed from them].

[Furthermore:]

» dedicating children [to Allāh ﷻ], castration, monasticism and anchoritism have been abrogated for them [i.e. the Muslims]. [It is reported] in a ḥadīth:

لَيْسَ فِيْ دِيْنِيْ تَرْكُ النِّسَاءِ، وَلَا اللَّحْمِ، وَلَا اتِّخَاذُ الصَّوَامِعِ

Abstinence from women and meat, and taking up hermitages, are not in my faith.[22]

If any of the Jews worked on a Saturday, he would be crucified; it has not been prescribed as such for us on a Friday.

[Furthermore, the previous Communities:]

» would not feed others until they had made *wuḍū'* like that of ritual prayer
» one who stole would be condemned to slavery
» one who committed suicide would be forbidden [entry into] Paradise
» when someone became their king, he would stipulate them to be his slaves, their properties to be his that he may take or leave what he wills.

[Legal Rights of His ﷺ Community]

[However:] they [i.e. the Muslims] have been given the legal right to:

» marry four wives
» three divorces
» the choice of marrying outside of their faith
» marry a bondmaid
» intimacy with the menstruating [wife], but not sexual relations
» approach the wife in any manner they choose.

---

22. Aṭ-Ṭabarī.

[Furthermore:]

» they have been given a legal right to choose between exacting retaliation (*qiṣāṣ*) or accepting compensatory payment (*diyah*)
» they have been given a legal right to repel the assailant; it was prescribed for the Banū Isrā'īl that when one man extended his hand [in aggression] to another man, the assailant would not be interfered with until he had either killed the latter or released him.

Mujāhid and Ibn Jurayj said this.

[Legal Restrictions on His ﷺ Community]

[Furthermore:] it has been prohibited for them [i.e. the Muslims] to:

» expose their private parts
» wail over the deceased
» form images
» drink intoxicants
» [use] instruments of amusement
» marry one's own sister
» [use] gold and silver utensils
» [wear] silk [for men]
» [wear] gold jewellery for their men
» prostrate to other than Allāh ﷻ; it was a greeting for those before us, but Allāh ﷻ has given us the [greeting of] salutation in its place
» fighting in battles is disapproved for them.

[Privileges for His ﷺ Community]

[Furthermore:] they have been protected from:

» collectively going astray
» the people of evil overcoming the people of good
» their Prophet ﷺ praying against them that they perish.

[Furthermore:]

» their scholarly consensus is a proof
» their mutual difference is mercy; the mutual difference of those prior to them was a punishment

» pestilence is a mercy and a testimony for them; it was a punishment for the [previous] communities
» whatever they [i.e. the Muslims] pray for, it will be answered.

[Honour of His ﷺ Community]

[Furthermore:]
» they [i.e. the Muslims] believe in the first Scripture [sent by Allāh ﷻ] and the last Book [sent by Allāh ﷻ]
» they make pilgrimage to the Sanctified House [in Makkah] – they do not perpetually stay away from it
» their sins are [also] forgiven by making *wuḍū'*
» [extra] ritual prayers remain as supererogatory for them
» they consume their own donations and are rewarded thereby
» reward in this world is hastened to them while it is also invested in the Hereafter
» the mountains and the trees are overjoyed when they [i.e. the Muslims] pass them by, by glorifying them and honouring them
» the gates of the heavens are opened up for their deeds and for their souls
» the angels are overjoyed with them
» Allāh ﷻ and His ﷻ angels send blessings upon them.

Sufyān ibn 'Uyaynah رحمه الله said: "Allāh ﷻ has honoured the Community of [Prophet] Muḥammad ﷺ; He ﷻ sends blessings upon them as He ﷻ sends blessings upon the Prophets عليهم السلام. He ﷻ has said:

هُوَ ٱلَّذِى يُصَلِّى عَلَيْكُمْ وَمَلَٰٓئِكَتُهُۥ

It is He who sends blessings upon you, as well as His angels[23]."

[Furthermore:]
» they [i.e. the Muslims] may die in their beds but yet they are [recorded as] martyrs with Allāh ﷻ
» the dining-spread is placed before them and they are forgiven before they wrap it up
» if any of them dons clothing, he is forgiven before he removes it.

23. Holy Qur'ān, Sūrat al-Aḥzāb (33), Verse 43.

[Furthermore:]

» their friend is the best of friends
» they [themselves] are wise scholars
» they could have all nearly become prophets due to their deep understanding
» for the sake of Allāh ﷻ, they do not fear reprimand by the blamer
» they are servile to the Believers; strong against the disbelievers
» their good deeds are the ritual prayer
» their sacrifice is their blood
» one whose deed is not accepted is concealed; prior to them, one whose immolation fire would not consume would be exposed
» their [i.e. the Muslims'] sins are forgiven through seeking forgiveness
» their being ashamed is akin to repenting.

Razīn said this.

It is reported that Prophet Ādam ﷺ said: "Allāh ﷻ has bestowed four privileges upon the Community of Muḥammad ﷺ that He ﷻ has not given to me; my repentance was made in Makkah whereas any of them may repent in all places; my clothing was removed from me when I erred but they are not stripped [of clothing]; a separation was affected between me and my wife; I was evicted from Paradise."

He [i.e. Razīn] said: "The Banū Isrā'īl would be forbidden good food if they made a mistake, and his mistake would be written upon the door of his house."

[Furthermore:] they [i.e. the Muslims] are promised that they shall not perish:

» out of hunger
» by a non-Muslim enemy who would seek to exterminate them
» by drowning
» by being punished with torment that those prior to them were subjected to.

[Furthermore:]

» Paradise is incumbent for any one servant [of Allāh ﷻ] if two of their [i.e. Muslim] witnesses testify in his favour; but in the previous communities [it was] if a hundred of them testified
» their [i.e. the Muslims'] deeds are relatively fewer but of a higher reward
» [Muslims are of] a shorter lifespan

» a man from the previous communities would worship thirty times more, but they [i.e. the Muslims] are better than him thirtyfold
» they have been bestowed with blessings, mercy and guidance during calamities
» they have been given knowledge of the first and the last
» the treasures of all things have been opened up for them, even [those of] knowledge
» they have been given chains of narration, lineages, declension, authoring of books, and preservation of the sunnah of their Prophet ﷺ.

Abū 'Alī al-Jayyānī said: "Allāh ﷻ has specified this Community with three things that He ﷻ has not given to anyone before them; i) chains of narration, ii) lineages, and iii) declension."

In the *Commentary on at-Tirmidhī*, Ibn al-'Arabī said: "None of the Communities that have ended at the starting of this Community ever had disposition of authorship and research, and nor did they enjoy any progress in specialisation and analysis during their existence."

In the *Commentary on al-Maḥṣūl*, al-Qarāfī said: "It is among his ﷺ unique particulars that an individual from his ﷺ Community may achieve such knowledge and understanding in a short lifespan that no-one from the previous Communities could achieve in a long lifespan."

He said: "It is thus that such knowledge, inventions and cognisances have been prepared for the distinguished jurists (*mujtahid*) of this Community, though their lifespans are relatively shorter."

Ends [al-Qarāfī's statement].

Qatādah said: "Allāh ﷻ has bestowed upon this Community:
» preservation of a thing that none among the previous communities was given – it is something that He ﷻ has specified this Community with, an honour that He ﷻ has honoured them by
» a group among them shall remain upon the Truth until the command of Allāh ﷻ comes to pass
» the earth shall never be devoid of a distinguished jurist among them who shall establish the proof of Allāh ﷻ – until time shall tumble with the shaking of foundations, and the major signs of the Last Hour appear."

[Furthermore:]

- at the culmination of every century, Allāh ﷻ shall send someone to them who shall reform the affairs of their religion for them – in the last century shall 'Īsā ibn Maryam ﷺ come
- among them [i.e. the Muslims], there are *Quṭbs*[24], *Awtād*[25], *Nujabā'*[26], and *Abdāl*[27]
- among them is one who shall lead 'Īsā ibn Maryam ﷺ in prayer
- among them are those who shall travel [swiftly] like the angels, being independent of food due to glorifying [Allāh ﷻ]
- they shall fight the Dajjāl
- their scholars are like the Prophets ﷺ of the Banū Isrā'īl
- in the heavens, the angels listen to their *adhān* and their *talbiyah* (Ḥajj chant).

[Furthermore:]

- they praise Allāh ﷻ (i.e. *al-ḥamdu li'Llāh*) in all circumstances
- they magnify [Allāh ﷻ] (i.e. *Allāhu Akbar*) upon all lofty places
- they glorify [Allāh ﷻ] (i.e. *subḥān Allāh*) in all low places
- when they wish something to happen, they say:

أَفْعَلَهُ إِنْ شَاءَ اللّٰهُ

If Allāh ﷻ wills, may He ﷻ make it happen

- when they are angry, they proclaim the oneness [of Allāh ﷻ] (i.e *lā ilāha illa'Llāh*)
- when they argue, they glorify [Allāh ﷻ] (i.e. *subḥān Allāh*)
- when they wish [to do something], they seek the best option from Allāh ﷻ and then they undertake it
- when they climb on to the backs of their mounts, they praise Allāh ﷻ
- their religious scriptures (i.e. the Qur'ān) are in their hearts
- the foremost among them are truly foremost – who shall enter Paradise without reckoning
- the middle among them are successful – who shall be judged with ease
- [even] the transgressors among them will be forgiven
- there is none among them who will not be showered with mercy
- they shall don the colours of the clothing of the inhabitants of Paradise.

24. pl. *aqṭāb* – poles of faith.
25. sing. *watad* – stake of faith.
26. sing. *najīb* – leader in faith.
27. sing. *badal* – substitute.

[Furthermore:]

» they observe the sun for ritual prayers
» they are the Community of Moderation (*Ummat Wasaṭ*)
» [they are] morally upright due to their purification by Allāh ﷻ
» the angels appear for them when they fight [in battles]
» whatever was obliged on the Prophets ﷺ and the Messengers ﷺ has been obliged on them, and that is *wuḍū'*, *ghusl* (ritual bathing) when ritually impure, Ḥajj (pilgrimage), and *jihād* (struggle)
» they have been given those supererogatory [aspects of worship] that were [only] given to Prophets ﷺ.

With regards to others, Allāh ﷻ said:

وَمِن قَوْمِ مُوسَىٰٓ أُمَّةٌ يَهْدُونَ بِٱلْحَقِّ وَبِهِۦ يَعْدِلُونَ

and among the people of Mūsā is a group who guide to the Truth and with it they do justice[28]

they [i.e. the Muslims] have been addressed in the Qur'ān with [the words]:

يَـٰٓأَيُّهَا ٱلَّذِينَ ءَامَنُوٓا۟

O you who believe![29]

whereas the [previous] Communities have been addressed in their scriptures [with the words]:

يَا أَيُّهَا الْمَسَاكِيْنُ

O you who are needy!

What a huge difference there is between both forms of address!

In the *Commentary on al-Minhāj*[30], ad-Damīrī[31] said: "Some scholars said: Allāh ﷻ has addressed this Community with the words:

فَٱذْكُرُونِىٓ أَذْكُرْكُمْ

So, remember Me and I shall remember you.[32]

He ﷻ commanded them to remember Him ﷻ without an intermediary, but He ﷻ instructed the Banū Isrā'īl in the words:

28. Holy Qur'ān, Sūrat al-A'rāf (7), Verse 159.
29. Holy Qur'ān, Sūrat al-Baqarah (2), Verse 254.
30. This is the commentary entitled *an-Najm al-Wahhāj fī Sharḥ al-Minhāj*. It is a commentary on Imām an-Nawawī's *Minhāj aṭ-Ṭālibīn*.
31. He is Muḥammad ibn Mūsā Kamāluddīn ad-Damīrī (744AH/1344CE – 807AH/ 1405CE).
32. Holy Qur'ān, Sūrat al-Baqarah (2), Verse 152.

يَٰبَنِىٓ إِسْرَٰٓءِيلَ ٱذْكُرُوا۟ نِعْمَتِىَ

O Banū Isrā'īl, remember my favour…[33]

They did not recognise Allāh ﷻ but through His ﷺ bounties, so He ﷻ commanded them to pursue the favours that they may reach through them the remembrance of the Provider of favours."

In *al-Khādim*, az-Zarkashī[34] said: "Whatever of noble traits and miracles were combined within him ﷺ, they were dispersed among his ﷺ Community. The evidence: verily, he ﷺ was free of sin, and therefore, the scholarly consensus of his ﷺ Community is [also] free of mistake."

Some said: "Thus, it is because he ﷺ has transferred his ﷺ secrets [to his ﷺ Community], and he ﷺ chose death [when] he ﷺ was given the options of life and death; and because Prophet Mūsā ؑ was not given that when the Angel of Death ؑ appeared to him ؑ, he ؑ slapped it."

The number of widows and slaves [among the Muslims] will be more than [those of] the other Communities.

In *Tafsīr Ibn Abū Ḥāṭim*, it was related by 'Ikrimah ؓ that he ؓ said: "There has never been a community wherein many races of people have entered, save for this Community."

[It is mentioned] in a ḥadīth when it was revealed:

وَٱلسَّٰبِقُونَ ٱلْأَوَّلُونَ مِنَ ٱلْمُهَٰجِرِينَ وَٱلْأَنصَارِ وَٱلَّذِينَ ٱتَّبَعُوهُم

بِإِحْسَٰنٍ رَّضِىَ ٱللَّهُ عَنْهُمْ وَرَضُوا۟ عَنْهُ

And the first of the foremost, among the Muhājirs (Migrants) and the Anṣār (Helpers), and those who followed them in good faith – Allah ﷻ is well pleased with them and they are well pleased with Him ﷻ,[35]

he ﷺ said: "This (i.e. pleasure of Allāh ﷻ) is for my Community – all of it. After pleasure there is no displeasure."

Mu'āwiyah ؓ said: "No community has ever differed [within itself] except that the supporters of evil among them have overcome the people of the Truth among them, save for this Community."

---

33. Holy Qur'ān, Sūrat al-Baqarah (2), Verse 122.
34. He is Badruddīn az-Zarkashī (d.794AH /1391CE).
35. Holy Qur'ān, Sūrat at-Tawbah (9), Verse 100.

In the *Commentary on ar-Risālah* of al-Jazūlī, it is said: "*Ahl al-Qiblah* (People of the Direction towards the Ka'bah) is a title with which the Community of Muḥammad ﷺ is specified."

In the *Sunan Abū Dāwūd*, [it is reported] in a ḥadīth:

لَنْ يَجْمَعَ اللهُ عَلَى هَذِهِ الأُمَّةِ سَيْفَيْنِ ، سَيْفًا مِنْهَا وَسَيْفًا مِنْ عَدُوِّهَا

Allāh ﷻ *will not gather two swords against this Community; a sword from among them and a sword from their enemy.*[36]

Ibn Mas'ūd ؓ said: "Stripping [others] of clothing, making the offender run when administering *ḥadd* punishment, malevolence and baseness are unlawful in this Community." This means that one's clothes are not to be stripped, and he is not made to run when being administered *ḥadd* punishment; rather, he is struck while he is sitting and while he is wearing his clothes.

[It is reported] in a ḥadīth:

لاَ تَرِثُ مِلَّةٌ مِلَّةً، وَلاَ تَجُوزُ شَهَادَةُ مِلَّةٍ عَلَى مِلَّةٍ إِلاَّ أُمَّةَ مُحَمَّدٍ صلى الله عليه وسلم، فَإِنَّ شَهَادَتَهُمْ تَجُوزُ عَلَى مَنْ سِوَاهُمْ

No community shall inherit another community, and the witnessing of one community over another community is not permitted except for the Community of Muḥammad ﷺ*; verily, their witnessing over others is allowed.*[37]

Ibn al-Jawzī said: "[In] the beginning, laws were based on making ease; burdening was not known in the laws of Prophet Nūḥ ﷺ, Prophet Ṣāliḥ ﷺ, and Prophet Ibrāhīm ﷺ. Thereafter, Prophet Mūsā ﷺ brought strictness and burdens, and Prophet 'Īsā ﷺ, likewise. Then, the Laws of our Prophet [Muḥammad] ﷺ brought an abrogation of the strictness of the People of the Scripture – they did not apply the absolute ease of those before them, but rather, they are in-between them."

Ends [Chapter 2].

36. Abū Dāwūd, *as-Sunan*, Chapter *Irtifā' al-Fitnah fi'l-Malāḥim*, Ḥadīth 4301.

37. 'Abdurrazzāq, *al-Muṣannaf*, Ḥadīth 15525; al-Hindī, *Kanz al-'Ummāl*, Ḥadīth 30437; al-Haythamī, *Majma' az-Zawā'id*, Ḥadith 7043.

CHAPTER

3

On what the Beloved Prophet Muḥammad ﷺ is personally specified with in the Hereafter.

[The Rising]

The Prophet Muḥammad ﷺ is specified in that:

» he ﷺ is the first for whom the earth shall split asunder [when he ﷺ rises from his ﷺ grave]
» he ﷺ is the first who shall recover from the thunderbolt
» he ﷺ shall enter the Plain of the Great Gathering (*Maḥshar*) in the company of seventy thousand angels
» he ﷺ shall enter the Plain of the Great Gathering (*Maḥshar*) [mounted] upon the Burāq
» he ﷺ shall be announced with his ﷺ name at the Station [in *Maḥshar*]
» he ﷺ shall be provided the best clothing of Paradise at the Station
» he ﷺ shall take position on the right side of the Divine Throne, at the Praised Station (*Maqām Maḥmūd*)
» the Standard of Praise shall be in his ﷺ hand
» Prophet Ādam عليه السلام and everyone else shall be under his ﷺ banner
» he ﷺ shall be the Imām of the Prophets عليهم السلام on that Day, as well as their leader and their sermoniser
» [he ﷺ shall be] the first to be allowed to prostrate
» the first to raise his ﷺ head
» the first to look towards Allāh ﷻ
» the first to intercede
» the first whose intercession shall be accepted
» he ﷺ shall ask for others whereas all the people will be asking for themselves.

[The Great Intercession]

[Furthermore, he ﷺ is specified with:]

» the Great Intercession with regards to judgement
» the intercession with regards to admitting the inhabitants of Paradise without reckoning
» the intercession with regards to someone who deserves [punishment in] the Fire [of Hell], that he is not entered therein
» the intercession in elevating the ranks of the people in Paradise

just as an-Nawawī has confirmed these particulars and those mentioned before them. Ḥadīths have been reported in reference to the aforementioned, whereas al-Qāḍī 'Iyāḍ and Ibn Diḥyah have been explicit about them.

[Furthermore, he ﷺ is specified with:]

» the intercession with regards to extracting the general populace of his ﷺ Community from the Fire [of Hell], until none remains therein.

As-Subkī has mentioned this.

[Furthermore, he ﷺ is specified with:]

» the intercession for a group of pious Muslims – so that their shortcomings in obedience [to Allāh ﷻ] may be overlooked.

Al-Qazwīnī has mentioned this in *al-'Urwat al-Wuthqā.*

[Furthermore, he ﷺ is specified with:]

» the intercession at the Station for ease on behalf of those who are being reckoned

» the intercession for the children of the polytheists that they are not punished

» his ﷺ asking his ﷺ Lord ﷻ not to enter any of his ﷺ household into the Fire [of Hell] and he ﷺ shall be granted that.

[Furthermore, he ﷺ is specified with:]

» the intercession for the non-Muslims who are perpetually in the Fire [of Hell] that their punishment is lessened for them.

[The Crossing into Paradise]

[Furthermore:]

» he ﷺ is the first who shall traverse the *Ṣirāṭ* (Bridge into Paradise)

» he ﷺ has light in each of the hairs of his ﷺ head and face; the [other] Prophets ﷩ were given only two lights

» the people in the gathering will be ordered to shut their eyes so that his ﷺ daughters may cross the *Ṣirāṭ.*

[Furthermore:]

» he ﷺ is the first who shall knock on the Gate of Paradise

» he ﷺ is the first who shall enter Paradise, followed by his ﷺ daughter.

[The River and the Fountain]

[Furthermore, he ﷺ is specified with:]

» the [River of] al-Kawthar.

Abū Saʿīd and Ibn Surāqah added: "… and the Fountain (*Ḥawḍ*)."

I said: "But it has been reported that there shall be a Fountain (*Ḥawḍ*) for every Prophet ﷺ."

[It has been mentioned] in a non-prophetic report (*athar*) on his ﷺ particulars [that]:

» his ﷺ Fountain (*Ḥawḍ*) is the most expansive and the most outflowing of all Fountains.

[Intermediacy]

[Furthermore, he ﷺ is specified with:]

» the intermediacy – this is the loftiest rank in Paradise.[38]

In *Shuʿab al-Īmān*, 'Abduljalīl al-Quṣayrī said: "The intermediacy that he ﷺ has been specified with is the 'being in the middle (*tawassul*)', and that is the Prophet ﷺ being like a minister in Paradise to the King ﷻ without himself ﷺ being represented. Nothing shall reach anyone but through his ﷺ intermediacy."

[His ﷺ Honours on the Day of Judgement]

[Furthermore, he ﷺ is specified with:]

» the supports of his ﷺ pulpit being firmly fixed in Paradise

» his ﷺ pulpit being upon one of the waterways of Paradise

» the space between his ﷺ grave and his ﷺ pulpit being a Garden from among the Gardens of Paradise

» no witness being sought to his ﷺ preaching [the religion of the Truth]; though it will be sought from all the other Prophets ﷺ and all the Prophets ﷺ will be witnessed to preaching [the religion of the Truth]

» all issues and ancestries being disconnected on the Day of Judgement except for his ﷺ issue and ancestry.

It is said: "This means that his ﷺ Community will be ascribed to him ﷺ on the Day of Judgement, but the Communities of all the other Prophets ﷺ will not be ascribed to them ﷺ."

38. Ibn Kathīr, *al-Bidāyah wa'n-Nihāyah*.

It is also said: "Ascription to him ﷺ shall be of benefit on that Day but all other ascriptions will not benefit. In Paradise, Prophet Ādam ﷺ will be given the filial appellation referring to him ﷺ rather than any of his ﷺ other descendants – out of honour to him ﷺ, and so he ﷺ will be called 'Abū Muḥammad'."

[Furthermore:]

» it has been mentioned in ḥadīths that the people of the prophetic interregnum (*fatrah*) between Prophet 'Īsā ﷺ and Prophet Muḥammad ﷺ will be put to the test on the Day of Judgement – whoever submitted in obedience shall enter Paradise, and whoever refused shall enter the Fire [of Hell].

Some of them [i.e. scholars] said: "It is presumed that all of the descendants of his ﷺ household shall submit in obedience at the test due to their proximity [in blood relationship] to him ﷺ."

[The Ranks of Paradise]

It has been reported [that]:

» the ranks of Paradise are equal to the number of the verses of the Qur'ān
» that it will be said to an inhabitant of Paradise: "Recite and proceed upwards"
» his final rank shall be at the last verse he recites
» nothing like this has been reported for any other Scripture.

Another unique particular comes forth from this:

» nothing but his ﷺ Book shall be recited in Paradise
» nothing shall be spoken in Paradise but his ﷺ language.

[The Praised Station]

In *Tafsīr Ibn Abū Ḥātim*, it has been reported by Sa'īd ibn Abū Hilāl: that it has reached him regarding the Praised Station, that on the Day of Judgement, the Messenger of Allāh ﷺ shall settle between the Magnificent Lord ﷻ and Angel Jibrīl ﷺ, and the entire assembly will envy him ﷺ due to that Station ﷺ.

[It is reported] in a ḥadīth:

أَنَا أَوَّلُ مَنْ يَقْرَعُ بَابَ الجنَّةِ، فَيَقُولُ الخَازِنُ: مَنْ أَنْتَ؟ فَأَقُولُ: أَنَا مُحَمَّدٌ.
فَيَقُولُ: أَقُومُ فأفْتَحُ لَكَ، فَلَمْ أَقُمْ لِأَحَدٍ قَبْلَكَ، وَلَا أَقُومُ لِأَحَدٍ بَعْدَكَ

I am the first who shall knock on the Gate of Paradise. The Gatekeeper will ask, "Who are you?" and I will respond, "I am Muḥammad." He will then say, "I shall stand and open it for you – I have never stood for anyone prior to you, and I shall never stand for anyone after you."[39]

[Ends Chapter 3.]

39. Muslim, *al-Musnad aṣ-Ṣaḥiḥ, Kitāb al-Īmān,* Ḥadīth 486.

CHAPTER

4

On what the Beloved Prophet Muḥammad ﷺ is specified with regarding his ﷺ Community in the Hereafter.

[The Community of Prophet Muḥammad 🕮 on the Day of Judgement]

It has been specified that his 🕮 Community shall:

» be the first among all Communities for whom the earth will split asunder [when they rise from their graves]

» come on the Day of Judgement with white blazes on their faces and on their limbs (*al-ghurr al-muḥajjalūn*) from the traces of *wuḍū'*

» be at the Station upon a high pile

» have two lights like the Prophets 🕮; others will have but one light

» have a mark on their faces from the trace of prostrations

» have their light rushing before them

» be handed their records in their right hands

» pass over the *Ṣirāṭ* like lightning and wind

» have their righteous people interceding for their ignoble people

» have their punishment awarded to them in this world and the *Barzakh* (Isthmus) so that they shall come purified on the Day of Judgement

» enter their graves with their sins but emerge from them sinless – their sins will be wiped out by the [other] Believers seeking forgiveness for them

» achieve what they strived for, and what was striven for them; those before them shall only have what they strived for.

[Rewards for His 🕮 Community]

'Ikrimah 🕮 said:

» "They shall be judged prior to any of the other creatures

» their sins committed unknowingly shall be forgiven

» of all people, they shall be the heaviest on the Scales (*Mīzān*)

» they shall attain the rank of equitable rulers

» they shall bear witness that the Messengers 🕮 had delivered [the message of Allāh 🕮] to them

» each one of them will be given a Jew or a Christian, and it shall be said to him: 'O Muslim! This is your ransom from the Fire [of Hell]'

» they shall enter Paradise prior to all of the other Communities

» seventy thousand of them shall enter Paradise without any reckoning

» all of their children will be in Paradise; this will not be the case with any of the other Communities – according to one of two bearings from as-Subkī in his exegesis [of the Qur'ān]."

Imām Fakhruddīn has stated: "The rewards shall be fewer of the Community of one ﷺ whose miracles are more evident."

As-Subkī said: "… except for this Community – the miracles of our Prophet ﷺ are most evident, but our rewards are more than [those of] all of the Communities.

The inhabitants of Paradise shall be of one hundred and twenty rows, of which this Community shall comprise eighty rows and the other communities of forty rows."

[Furthermore:]

» Allāh ﷻ will reveal Himself ﷻ to them [i.e. the Muslims], and they will behold Him ﷻ

» they will prostrate to Him ﷻ – according to the [scholarly] consensus of the People of the Sunnah (*Ahlu's-Sunnah*); as for the previous Communities, there are two possibilities – according to Ibn Abū Jamrah [whether they shall see Allāh ﷻ or not].

In *Fawā'id* of al-Qāḍī Abu'l-Ḥusayn ibn al-Muhtadī, there is a *marfū'* (traced back to the Prophet Muḥammad ﷺ) ḥadīth reported by Ibn 'Umar رضي الله عنهما:

كُلُّ أُمَّةٍ بَعْضُهَا فِي الْجَنَّةِ وَبَعْضُهَا فِي النَّارِ إِلَّا هَذِهِ الْأُمَّةَ فَإِنَّهَا كُلُّهَا فِي الْجَنَّةِ

[From] all communities, some will be in Paradise and some will be in the Fire (of Hell), except for this Community; all of it will be in Paradise.

It has been reported by ar-Rab'ī in the *Muṣannaf* of 'Abdurrazzāq that he read in some of the books that an illegitimate child shall not enter Paradise, up to seven ancestral generations, but Allāh ﷻ gave ease to this Community and reduced it to five generations.

[Ends Chapter 4.]

PART

2

On the unique particulars the Beloved Prophet Muḥammad ﷺ is specified with from his ﷺ Community, some of which the Prophets ﷺ are known to share with him ﷺ, and some of which are not known.

It has four chapters.

- [Chapter 1: On what the Beloved Prophet Muḥammad ﷺ is specified with regarding obligations.
- Chapter 2: On what the Beloved Prophet Muḥammad ﷺ is specified with regarding proscriptions.
- Chapter 3: On what the Beloved Prophet Muḥammad ﷺ is specified with regarding the lawful.
- Chapter 4: On what the Beloved Prophet Muḥammad ﷺ is specified with regarding honours and merits.]

CHAPTER 1

On what the Beloved Prophet Muḥammad ﷺ is specified with regarding obligations. The wisdom behind it is an increase in proximity and degrees.

[What Prophet Muḥammad ﷺ is Obligated With]

The Prophet Muḥammad ﷺ is specified with being obligated with:

» the ritual prayer:
at Mid-Morning (*Ṣalāt aḍ-Ḍuḥā*)
that which is Odd-Numbered (*Ṣalāt al-Witr*), and
at Late Night (*Ṣalāt at-Tahajjud*), i.e. the ritual prayer performed at night
» brushing the teeth
» sacrificing [an animal]
» mutual consultation – according to the most correct opinion
» two units of prayer at *fajr* – according to the ḥadīth in *al-Mustadrak*, etc.

[Furthermore:]

» bathing on Fridays – according to a ḥadīth
» four units of ritual prayer at midday – according to what has been reported by Sa'īd ibn al-Musayyib ﷺ.

[Furthermore:]

» it is said: "*wuḍū'* prior to every prayer," but then it was abrogated
» *wuḍū'* as soon as he ﷺ nullifies it – [in which case] he ﷺ must neither speak to anyone and nor respond to salutations until he ﷺ has made *wuḍū'* – but then it was abrogated
» it is said: "seeking the protection [of Allāh ﷻ] (i.e. *isti'ādhah*) when reciting [the Qur'ān]"
» being steadfast against the enemy even if their number be vast
» not to cease pursuing a man he ﷺ encounters in battle until he ﷺ slays him
» altering that which is denied – the reason of its being specific to him ﷺ is that:

a. it is from among the obligations of faith (*īmān*), but with regards to others it is from among the communal obligations. Al-Jurjānī has mentioned this in *ash-Shāfī*.
b. it is obliged upon him ﷺ to express denial, but such expression is not obliged on his ﷺ Community. The author of *adh-Dhakhā'ir* has mentioned this.
c. it does not lapse from him ﷺ even in fear because Allāh ﷻ has promised protection to him ﷺ, as opposed to others. This is mentioned in *ar-Rawḍah*.
d. and nor when denial increases incitement in the perpetrator – so that it is not perceived as being permissible. [This is an obligation upon the Prophet Muḥammad ﷺ,] as opposed to the whole Community.

As-Sam'ānī has mentioned this in *al-Qawāṭi'*.

[His ﷺ Distinctions from His ﷺ Community]

[Furthermore, he ﷺ is distinguished from his ﷺ Community by:]

» his ﷺ fulfilment of promises being obligatory is equal to the surety of others, as opposed to the entire Community.

Al-Jawzī, and a group [of scholars] have mentioned this.

[Furthermore, he ﷺ is obliged to:]

» furnish the debt of a Muslim who dies impoverished – according to the most correct opinion.

[Rights of His ﷺ Wives]

[Furthermore, he ﷺ is obliged to:]

» allow his ﷺ wives to separate from him ﷺ or remain with him ﷺ – according to the most correct opinion

» keep them if they choose to stay with him ﷺ – according to one of two opinions

» refrain from marrying when in wedlock to them

» and from substituting them [for others] – as a recompense to them. This was later abrogated, so that it would be a favour from him ﷺ [to them].

[Further Obligations on Him ﷺ]

[Furthermore, the Prophet Muḥammad ﷺ is specifically obligated to:]

» say:

لَبَّيْكَ ، إِنَّ الْعَيْشَ عَيْشُ الْآخِرَةِ

Here I am, (O Lord)! Verily, the real life is the life of the Hereafter[40]

» when impressed by something. It has been originally narrated in *ar-Rawḍah* in another perspective:

» perform obligatory prayer perfectly and without any deficiency therein.

Al-Māwardī and others have mentioned this:

» complete every supererogatory act of worship that he ﷺ commences.

It has been originally narrated in *ar-Rawḍah*:

» respond with that which is better.

---

40. Al-Bukhārī, *al-Jāmi' aṣ-Ṣaḥīḥ, Kitāb al-Jihād wa's-Siyar*, Ḥadīth 2834; *Kitāb al-Maghāzī*, Ḥadīth 4099. Similar ḥadīths are found in other books of Prophetic Narrations.

[His ﷺ Being Distinguished from the Rest of the Created Beings]

[Furthermore, he ﷺ is distinguished from the rest of the created beings because:]

» he ﷺ alone is assigned knowledge that the entire humanity has collectively been assigned

» he ﷺ was invited to behold the Beatific Vision while physically living among the people and conversing [with them].

Ibn Sabʿ and Ibn al-Qāṣṣ have mentioned the [last] three in *at-Talkhīṣ*.

In *Sharaf al-Muṣṭafā*, Abū Saʿīd said: "He ﷺ was commissioned with such works that all of the people have been commissioned with, though there is much difference between both affairs – he ﷺ would be separated from the world during the Revelation, but fasting, ritual prayer, and all the rulings would not lapse from him ﷺ."

Ibn al-Qāṣṣ and al-Qaffāl have mentioned this in *Zawā'id ar-Rawḍah*, and Ibn Sabʿ has acknowledged it.

[His ﷺ Seeking Forgiveness from Allāh ﷻ]

[Furthermore, he ﷺ is distinguished from his ﷺ Community because:]

» he ﷺ seeks the forgiveness of Allāh ﷻ seventy times whenever his ﷺ heart is influenced with desire.

Ibn al-Qāṣṣ has mentioned this and Ibn al-Mulaqqan has cited it in *al-Khaṣā'iṣ*.

The text of Abū Saʿīd from *Sharaf al-Muṣṭafā* reads: "He ﷺ would seek the forgiveness of Allāh ﷻ seventy times every day even though he ﷺ would not sin."

The text of Razīn in his *Khaṣā'iṣ* reads: "Among his ﷺ obligations is that he ﷺ seeks the forgiveness of Allāh ﷻ seventy times every day."

[His ﷺ Ritual Prayers]

[Furthermore, he ﷺ is distinguished from his ﷺ Community because:]

» there were two units [of prayer] obligatory on him ﷺ after the *ʿaṣr* prayer

» all of his ﷺ supererogatory prayers were obligatory [in status] – because supererogatory acts are to compensate [for losses], but there was no deficiency in his ﷺ ritual prayer for them to compensate.

He ﷺ is specified with:

- » fifty ritual prayers [as a reward] for each prayer performed during each day and night – in accordance with what took place on the Night when he ﷺ was taken on the Night Journey (*Laylat al-Isrā'*). Ḥadīths have been mentioned with regards to his ﷺ ritual prayers reaching a hundred units, besides the five [daily obligatory ritual prayers]
- » he ﷺ would wake anyone he ﷺ would ever pass by who was sleeping during the time for prayer. This is in conformity to the saying of Allāh ﷻ:

أُدْعُ إِلَىٰ سَبِيلِ رَبِّكَ

(*O Beloved Messenger* ﷺ) *Call to the way of your Lord.*[41]

He [i.e. Razīn] said: "He ﷺ is specified in that it is obligatory on him ﷺ to:

- » perform *'aqīqah* (sacrifice an animal on the occasion of a child's birth)
- » repay a gift
- » be harsh on the rejecters [of the Truth]
- » encourage the Muslims to fight [in defence].

[Other Obligations for Him ﷺ and on Him ﷺ]

[Furthermore, he ﷺ is distinguished from his ﷺ Community because:]

- » it is obligatory to trust him ﷺ
- » hoarding is forbidden for him ﷺ.

[Furthermore:]

- » he ﷺ would provide for the family of one who died poor
- » pay the penalty fines for one liable and poor – as well as for [their] expiations.

[He ﷺ is specified in that] it is obligatory on him ﷺ to:

- » be patient upon what is undesirable
- » be patient with himself ﷺ upon those who call upon their Lord ﷻ in the morning and at night
- » be gentle and avoid harshness
- » preach all that is revealed to him ﷺ
- » address the people according to what they understand
- » supplicate for whoever gives in charity out of his wealth.

41. Holy Qur'ān, Sūrat an-Naḥl (16), Verse 125.

It is said: 'If there was anything that would lead to proximity with Allāh ﷻ, it was obliged upon him ﷺ.'

[Furthermore, it is obligatory on him ﷺ to:]

» never make a promise nor delay a matter to the next day without separating it."

What has been related by Razīn, ends.

Abū Sa'īd said: "It was obliged on him ﷺ to protect the property of Muslims."

Leading ritual prayer (*imāmah*) was more excellent for him ﷺ than calling the *adhān* – according to one reason stated by al-Jurjānī in *ash-Shāfī* is because he ﷺ, contrary to other people, would never concede to forgetfulness or error. It is necessary to stop here, as it is a point of difference for other people, regarding the superiority between leading ritual prayer and calling the *adhān*.

Some of the Ḥanafī [scholars] have mentioned: "The obligation to perform funeral prayer (*janāzah*) in his ﷺ time would not lapse unless he ﷺ performed it." This is interpreted as funeral prayer being a personal obligation upon him ﷺ but a communal obligation upon others.

[Ends Chapter 1.]

CHAPTER

2

On what the Beloved Prophet Muḥammad ﷺ is specified with regarding proscriptions.

[Property That is Prohibited for Prophet Muḥammad ﷺ]

He ﷺ is specified that:

» [property gained from] *zakāh* (mandatory poor-due), charity and expiations are [all] prohibited for him ﷺ
» *zakāh* is prohibited for his ﷺ descendants. It is said: "charity as well," and the Mālikī [scholars] are of this opinion
» [*zakāh* is prohibited] for the slaves of his ﷺ household – according to the most correct opinion
» upon his wives – according to scholarly consensus.

Ibn 'Abdulbarr has stated this.

» [Prohibited is] also [the property gained from] vows.

Al-Bulqīnī said: "It is taken from this that it was forbidden for something to be donated specifically to him ﷺ because donations are supererogatory charity."

He said: "What supports this is mentioned in *al-Jawāhir* by al-Qamūlī, and he said: '[Property gained from] supererogatory charity was prohibited for him ﷺ, according to the most correct opinion.'"

It was reported by Ibn Abū Hurayrah ﷺ that specific charity is prohibited for him ﷺ but not general charity, such as masjids, digging wells, etc.

Working as administrators of *zakāh* is prohibited for his ﷺ household – according to the most correct opinion.

[Furthermore, it is prohibited to:]

» pay vows and expiations to them [i.e. the Prophetic Household]
» consume the property of any of the descendants of Prophet Isma'īl ﷺ. A ḥadīth has been mentioned in this regard in *al-Musnad* [of Imām Aḥmad], and I did not find anything opposing it
» consuming that which is malodorous
» eating while reclining – according to one of two claims.

The most accurate opinion mentioned in *ar-Rawḍah* is the [aforementioned] two being disapproved.

Abū Sa'īd, in *Sharaf al-Muṣṭafā*, said: "The dab lizard is disapproved [for him ﷺ]."

[Poetry and Writing is Prohibited for Him ﷺ]

[Furthermore:]

» scribing and making poetry is prohibited for him ﷺ

Al-Māwardī said: "This is how it has been reported."

» reading from a written text [is prohibited for him ﷺ].

In *at-Tahdhīb*, al-Baghawī said: "It is said: 'He ﷺ could write beautifully but he ﷺ did not; he ﷺ could make wonderful poetry but he ﷺ did not.' However, the most accurate opinion is that he ﷺ would do neither of them well, though he ﷺ would distinguish between fine and inferior poetry."

[Aspects of War being Prohibited for Him ﷺ]

[Furthermore, it is prohibited for him ﷺ:]

» once he ﷺ had put it on, to remove his ﷺ armour until he ﷺ had fought with it in battle or that Allāh ﷻ had decided between him ﷺ and his ﷺ enemy. This was the same [ruling] for the [other] Prophets ﷺ.

Abū Sa'īd and Ibn Surāqah said: "He ﷺ would not turn back once he ﷺ had set off for battle. He ﷺ would not be defeated when he ﷺ encountered the enemy, even if their number overwhelmed him ﷺ."

[Other Prohibitions for Him ﷺ]

[Furthermore, it is prohibited for him ﷺ:]

» to do favours in order to seek more for himself ﷺ. This means that he ﷺ would not give a gift to gain more back from it

» to indicate with the eyes towards that which the people consider a luxury of the mundane life of this world

» to express treacherous eyes (*khā'inat al-a'yun*). This is to indicate in such a manner towards that which is permitted, such as [legally sanctioned] killing or beating, as is against the apparent. This was the same [ruling] for the [other] Prophets ﷺ.

[Furthermore, it is prohibited for him ﷺ:]

» to deceive in battle – according to what Ibn al-Qāṣṣ has mentioned, but the majority have opposed him

» to perform the [funeral] prayer for a debtor. This was later abrogated.

[Issues Pertaining to His ﷺ Marriage]

[Furthermore, it is prohibited for him ﷺ:]

» to keep a woman [as his ﷺ wife] who disliked him ﷺ. According to one of two opinions, she was prohibited to him ﷺ forever

» to marry a woman who had not migrated – according to one of two reports

» to marry a woman from among the People of the Scripture. It is said: "… as well as keeping her as a bondmaid."

» to marry a Muslim bondmaid. If he ﷺ could marry a bondmaid and his ﷺ child born from her being free, paying [the master] for it would not be incumbent on the Prophet ﷺ, and in such a case it would not be stipulated for him ﷺ to have committed a wrong nor would have *ṭawl al-ḥurrah* (capacity to marry a freewoman) been compromised. He ﷺ may have more than one [bondmaid].

Imām al-Ḥaramayn said: "If he ﷺ was to marry [a bondmaid] by mistake, paying [the master] for the child would not be incumbent on him ﷺ."

Ibn ar-Rafʿah said: "Even thinking of that about him ﷺ is not [a matter] settled upon."

Al-Bulqīnī said: "His ﷺ being pushed to marrying a bondmaid can never be thought of. Even if a bondmaid appealed to him ﷺ, it would be obliged on her master to offer her to him ﷺ as a gift – as an analogy to food."

If he ﷺ sent a marriage proposal and it was rejected, he ﷺ would not resend it. This is how it is [mentioned] in a *mursal* (expedited) ḥadīth, as it bears prohibition and disapproval, as an analogy to keeping a woman [as his ﷺ wife] who dislikes him ﷺ. I did not find anything opposing this.

Ibn Sabʿ has enumerated among his ﷺ unique particulars:

» prohibition to attack [the enemy in battle] after he ﷺ had heard the *adhān*.

[What He ﷺ Would Refrain from Doing]

Al-Quḍāʿī and others have enumerated among his ﷺ unique particulars that:

» he ﷺ would not accept gifts from those who associated partners with Allāh ﷻ

» he ﷺ would not seek their assistance

» he ﷺ would not bear witness for injustice.

It was prohibited for him ﷺ to consume alcohol from the very beginning of [his ﷺ] prophethood, prior to it being forbidden to the people by approximately twenty years. It was never permitted to him ﷺ. [It is mentioned] in a ḥadīth:

أَوَّلُ مَا نَهَانِي عَنْهُ رَبِّي بَعْدَ عِبَادَةِ الْأَوْثَانِ شُرْبُ الْخَمْرِ وَمُلَاحَاةُ الرِّجَالِ

The first thing my Lord forbade me after idol-worship was drinking wine and being candid with the people.[42]

"I was prohibited from making myself naked and from revealing my private parts fifty years prior to my announcing prophethood."

Lady 'Ā'ishah ﷺ said: "I did not see his ﷺ [private parts] and he ﷺ did not see mine."

He ﷺ specifically forbade 'Alī ﷺ from having a donkey mate with a horse. Razīn mentioned this.

He ﷺ would not pray the funeral of one who broke trusts and nor of one who committed suicide. In *al-Mustadrak*, it is reported from Abū Qatādah who said:

كَانَ النَّبِيُّ صَلَّى اللهُ عَلَيْهِ وَآلِهِ وَسَلَّمَ إِذَا دُعِيَ إِلَى جَنَازَةٍ سَأَلَ عَنْهَا، فَإِنْ أُثْنِيَ عَلَيْهَا خَيْرٌ صَلَّى عَلَيْهَا ، وَإِنْ أُثْنِيَ عَلَيْهَا غَيْرُ ذَلِكَ قَالَ لِأَهْلِهَا : شَأْنُكُمْ بِهَا - وَلَمْ يُصَلِّ عَلَيْهَا

Whenever the Prophet ﷺ was called to a funeral, he ﷺ would ask about the deceased. If it was praised, he ﷺ would pray (the funeral prayer) over it, and if it was not praised, he ﷺ would say to its family, "You deal with it," and he ﷺ would not pray over it.[43]

In *Sunan Abū Dāwūd* is a ḥadīth:

مَا أُبَالِي مَا أَتَيْتُ إِنْ أَنَا شَرِبْتُ تِرْيَاقاً أَوْ تَعَلَّقْتُ تَمِيمَةً أَوْ قُلْتُ الشِّعْرَ مِنْ قِبَلِ نَفْسِي

I shall be one who does not care what he does if I drink an antidote, tie an amulet or compose poetry from myself.

42. Ibn Mājah, *as-Sunan*; aṭ-Ṭabarānī, *al-Mu'jam al-Awsaṭ*.
43. Al-Ḥākim, *al-Mustadrak*.

Abū Dāwūd said: “This is specific to the Prophet ﷺ, as drinking an antidote has been permitted to other people.”

Ends [Abū Dāwūd’s statement].

Tying amulets has been permitted for other people, provided it is after a calamity has befallen.

[Ends Chapter 2.]

CHAPTER

3

On what the Beloved Prophet Muḥammad ﷺ is specified with regarding the lawful.

[Ritual Purity of Prophet Muḥammad ﷺ]

He ﷺ is specified with:

» the lawfulness to remain inside the masjid in a state of major ritual impurity (*junub*). He ﷺ may pass through it – according to the Mālikī [scholars]
» that his ﷺ ablution does not break with sleeping or by touching a woman – according to one of two opinions, and this is the more correct.

[His ﷺ Facing When Answering Nature's Call]

[Furthermore,] it is said: "[He ﷺ is specified with] the permissibility to face the direction of the Ka'bah (*Qiblah*) and turning his ﷺ back to it when answering the call of nature." Ibn Daqīq al-'Īd mentioned this in the *Commentary on al-'Umdah*.

[His ﷺ Ritual Prayers]

[Furthermore, he ﷺ is specified with] the permissibility to:

» offer ritual prayer after [the ritual prayer of] *'aṣr*
» perform missed ritual prayers after [the ritual prayer of] *'aṣr* – according to one group [of scholars]
» carry an infant girl while performing ritual prayer – according to what some [scholars] have stated
» perform the funeral prayer over an absent body – according to Abū Ḥanīfah, and at the grave – according to the Mālikī [scholars].

[Furthermore, he ﷺ is specified with the permissibility to:]

» perform the odd-numbered ritual prayer (*ṣalāt al-witr*) while mounted, even though the odd-numbered ritual prayer (*ṣalāt al-witr*) is incumbent (*wājib*) on him ﷺ.

This is mentioned in the *Commentary on al-Muhadhdhab*:

» and also seated.

This is mentioned in *al-Khādim*:

» he ﷺ would recite in it audibly as well as inaudibly.

[Furthermore, he ﷺ is specified with the permissibility to:]

» lead the ritual prayer seated – according to what one group [of scholars] has mentioned

» appoint a substitute for himself ﷺ in leading ritual prayer – as took place with Abū Bakr رضي الله عنه when he ﷺ himself moved back and placed him رضي الله عنه ahead – according to what one group [of scholars] has said
» for him ﷺ to perform a portion of the same unit of ritual prayer standing and a portion of it sitting – according to what some of the predecessors have mentioned. They said: "It is forbidden for others."

[His ﷺ Other Privileges]

[He ﷺ is specified with the permissibility to:]
» kiss while fasting even though his ﷺ sexual desire to have sexual relations would be strong
» brush his ﷺ teeth while fasting after the sun's decline from the meridian.
Razīn has mentioned this.

It is said: "[He ﷺ is permitted] to fast while in the state of major ritual impurity." Aṭ-Ṭaḥāwī mentioned this.

[Furthermore, he ﷺ is specified with] the permissibility to:
» enter Makkah while not being in the state of *Iḥrām* (ritual proscription)
» repeatedly wear perfume while in the state of *Iḥrām* – according to what the Mālikī [scholars] have mentioned
» take the food or drink of any one he ﷺ wishes.
» Razīn added: "… and [take] his clothing if he ﷺ needs it."

[Furthermore,] it is obliged on the owner to:
» offer [his property to the Prophet ﷺ] even if he himself may perish
» sacrifice his being for the being of the Messenger of Allāh ﷺ.

[Pertaining to Marriage]

[Furthermore, he ﷺ is specified with] the permissibility to:
» look towards marriageable females, be in seclusion with them, seat them behind him on mounts
» marry more than four women [simultaneously]. This was the same [ruling] for the [other] Prophets عليهم السلام
» marry:

using the word '*hibah* – gift'
without dowry at the beginning or the ending
with an unknown dowry. Ar-Rūyānī stated this in *al-Baḥr*
without a guardian (*walī*)
without witnesses
in the state of *Iḥrām*
without the consent of the woman.

If he ﷺ is inclined to marry a woman who is single and available for marriage, it is binding upon her to accept [his ﷺ proposal] and it shall be forbidden for anyone else to propose marriage to her due to the inclination alone. If she is married, it is binding upon her husband to divorce her so that the Prophet ﷺ may marry her.

Al-Ghazālī said: "In such a case, it is permitted for him ﷺ to marry her prior to the completion of her waiting period (*'iddah*)."

[Furthermore:]
» he ﷺ may propose marriage to someone who has already been proposed to by someone else
» he ﷺ may marry a woman to anyone he ﷺ wants without her permission or without the permission of her guardian
» he ﷺ may compel a minor female [to marry], in addition to his ﷺ own daughters. He ﷺ gave in marriage the daughter of [his ﷺ uncle] Ḥamzah ﷺ in the presence of her paternal uncle 'Abbās رضي الله عنه, and he ﷺ thereby stepped ahead of the closest relative.

He ﷺ said to Umm Salamah رضي الله عنها:

مُرِيْ اِبْنَكِ أَنْ يُزَوِّجَكِ، فَزَوَّجَهَا اِبْنُهَا سَلَمَةُ بْنُ أَبِيْ سَلَمَةَ مِنْ رَسُوْلِ اللهِ
صَلَّى اللهُ عَلَيْهِ وَسَلَّمَ وَهُوَ غُلَامٌ لَمْ يَبْلُغْ

Tell your son to marry you (away). Thus, her son – Salamah ibn Abū Salamah رضي الله عنه married her (away) to the Messenger of Allāh ﷺ, even though he رضي الله عنه was a child who had not attained majority.

Allāh ﷻ married him ﷺ to Zaynab رضي الله عنها, and he ﷺ entered upon her رضي الله عنها due to the marriage done by Allāh ﷻ and without [formal] wedlock.

In *ar-Rawḍah*, this has been interpreted with the words: "Any woman was lawful for him ﷺ due to the legalisation by Allāh ﷻ."

In *Sharaf al-Muṣṭafā*, Abū Sa'īd said: "He ﷺ was suitable in marriage for everyone. It was permitted for him ﷺ if he ﷺ was married to by a guardian who is openly disobedient, blind or mute."

Ends [Abū Sa'īd's statement].

[Furthermore,] he ﷺ may:

» marry away to someone a woman who is in her waiting period (*'iddah*). This is weak according to one saying. This is what *ar-Rāfi'ī* has related

» combine [by marriage] a woman and her sister; her paternal aunt; her maternal aunt – according to one of two opinions; a woman and her daughter – according to one saying that *ar-Rāfi'ī* related.

In his *al-Khaṣā'iṣ*, Razīn said: "If he ﷺ has sexual relations with a lawfully acquired bondmaid, unlawfulness with regards to her mother, her daughter or her sister will not be ruled, if combining them is prohibited [for him ﷺ at all]."

Ends [Razīn's statement].

It is possible that this may be the claim mentioned in *ash-Sharḥ* and *ar-Rawḍah*, and it is also possible that it may be something else such that he may have differed between a wife and a bondmaid.

His ﷺ freeing his ﷺ bondmaid and her being manumitted is her dowry. He ﷺ freed the prisoners-of-war belonging to the tribe of Juwayriyah رضي الله عنها as dowry for her رضي الله عنها.

[Furthermore, he ﷺ is specified with the permissibility to:]

» marry a female who has not reached majority – according to what Ibn Shibramah has stated, but scholarly consensus is opposed to it

» omit the apportionment [of time] between his ﷺ wives – according to one of two opinions, and this is the preferred opinion.

In the *Commentary on at-Tirmidhī*, Ibn al-'Arabī said: "Allāh ﷻ has rendered some actions in marriage specific to His ﷻ Prophet ﷺ, which include:

i. He ﷻ has given to him ﷺ a moment wherein none of his ﷺ of wives have any right [over him ﷺ], such that he ﷺ can enter upon any of his ﷺ wives and do whatever he ﷺ wants, and thereafter enter upon the one whose turn it would be."

ii. it is not incumbent on him ﷺ to pay their maintenance – according to one saying, just like dowry. He ﷺ is not under any obligation.
iii. his ﷺ divorcement is not confined to three – according to one of two opinions. As for the confinement, it is said: "She would be lawful for him ﷺ without the legalisation of remarriage process (*ḥalālah*)," and it is also said: "She would never be lawful for him [again]."
iv. giving the choice [of divorce] to his ﷺ wives is explicit [for him ﷺ] – according to one opinion, whereas it is definitely implied for other people. With the explicit [choice of divorce], she would be divorced [with a] final [divorce] being eternally unlawful [to him ﷺ] – according to one opinion, as opposed to anyone else.

The reference of these unique particulars of the Prophet ﷺ with regards to marriage are like our having bondmaids. If he ﷺ rendered a bondmaid unlawful to himself ﷺ, she would not become unlawful and neither would he ﷺ be liable to expiate.

[Spoils of War]

[Furthermore,] he ﷺ may:

» exclude [something] in his ﷺ statement with a pause
» choose whatever he ﷺ wants from spoils [of war] prior to distribution, such as a bondmaid, etc., and likewise *fay'*-booty. Ibn Kuj mentioned this in *at-Tajrīd*.
» [choose] five-fifths the spoils [of war], as well as
» four-fifths of *fay'*-booty
» he ﷺ may do as he ﷺ wishes with the spoils of war.

Mālik, in his *Khaṣā'iṣ* [of the Prophet ﷺ] mentioned: "He ﷺ would not own spoils [of war]; he ﷺ would only have power of disposition in it and only take according to his ﷺ need."

According to ash-Shāfi'ī and others, he ﷺ would take ownership.

He ﷺ may take barren [ownerless] land for himself ﷺ, and his ﷺ ownership of what he ﷺ takes shall never end. However, whoever takes anything that he ﷺ owns shall be liable to pay for it – according to the most correct opinion, as opposed to what other leaders own. [Nevertheless,] if someone powerful takes it into custody, nothing shall be due on him.

[Battles, etc.]

[Furthermore, he ﷺ is specified with the permissibility to:]

» do battle in Makkah
» carry weapons [therein] and fight with them
» slay after giving sanctuary [to someone]
» curse without due cause whom he ﷺ wills – which would be a mercy for that person
» adjudicate based on his ﷺ own knowledge; this is differed upon with regards to other people
» [adjudicate] for himself ﷺ or for his ﷺ child
» bear witness for himself ﷺ or for his ﷺ child
» accept the witnessing of someone in his ﷺ own favour or the favour of his ﷺ child
» accept gifts; as opposed to other rulers.

[His ﷺ Legislative Powers]

» It is not disapproved for him ﷺ to issue edicts and make decisions in anger. An-Nawawī mentioned this in the *Commentary on Muslim*.
» If he ﷺ says: "So-and-so owes such-and-such to so-and-so," it shall be permitted for the listener to be a witness to that. Shurayḥ and ar-Rūyānī mentioned this in *Rawḍat al-Ḥukkām*.
» He ﷺ may slay whom he ﷺ accuses without evidence of him having committed unlawful sexual intercourse. This is not permitted for anyone else. Ibn Diḥyah mentioned this.
» He ﷺ can supplicate for anyone he ﷺ wishes using the words '*aṣ-ṣalāh* – blessings'; we are not allowed to send blessings [using the words '*aṣ-ṣalāh*'] except to a Prophet ﷺ or an angel ﷺ.
» He ﷺ made devotional sacrifice on behalf of his ﷺ Community; it is impermissible for anyone to make devotional sacrifice on behalf of anyone else without his authorisation.
» He ﷺ ate from unexpected food while forbidding it. Ibn al-Qāṣṣ mentioned this, but al-Bayhaqī denied it and said: "Verily, it is permitted for the Community because prohibition has not been established."
» He ﷺ may combine himself ﷺ and Allāh ﷻ using one [and the same] pronoun. Ibn 'Abdussalām and others have mentioned this.

» He ﷺ may slay anyone who insults him ﷺ or mocks him ﷺ. Ibn Sab' has enumerated this.
» He ﷺ would apportion the lands prior to having conquered them – because Allāh ﷻ had made him ﷺ the owner of the entire earth.

Al-Ghazālī decreed disbelief of anyone who disputes with the descendants of Tamīm ad-Dārī ﷺ in relation to what he ﷺ had apportioned to them, and he [i.e. al-Ghazālī] said: "He ﷺ would apportion the lands of Paradise, whereas he ﷺ is a degree superior with regards to the lands of this world."

In *at-Tanwīr*, Shaykh Tājuddīn ibn 'Aṭā'ullāh has mentioned: "The payment of *zakāh* is not obligatory on Prophets ﷺ as:

i. they have no property besides attachment to Allāh ﷻ. They would gift away whatever they would possess as endowments belonging to Allāh ﷻ, donating it where it is appropriately donatable and withholding it from inappropriate avenues of spending;
ii. *zakāh* is a purifier for whom it may be due on, whereas the Prophets ﷺ are free of impurities due to their innocence."

He ﷺ entered into an agreement of cropsharing by irrigation (*musāqāh*) with the people of Khaybar for an unknown duration by his ﷺ saying:

أُقِرُّكُمْ مَا أَقَرَّكُمُ اللّٰهُ بِهِ

I endorse for you what Allāh ﷻ has endorsed for you[44]

because the Revelation to abrogate was possible, though that would not have happened after him ﷺ.

He ﷺ swore an oath not to give any means of conveyance to the Ash'arīs, but then he ﷺ did give to them means of conveyance, and he ﷺ said:

لَسْتُ أَنَا حَمَلْتُكُمْ، وَلَكِنَّ اللّٰهَ حَمَلَكُمْ

It is not I who has given you the means of conveyance but Allāh ﷻ has given you the means of conveyance[45]

and no violation of oath has occurred or expiation due.

He ﷺ embraced Ja'far ﷺ when he ﷺ arrived from the journey, and so Mālik said: "It is specific to him ﷺ," and he disapproved it for others.

44. Al-Bukhārī, *al-Jāmi' aṣ-Ṣaḥīḥ*, *Kitāb al-Jizyah wa'l-Muwāda'ah*, Ḥadīth 3167.
45. Al-'Asqalānī, *Fatḥ al-Bārī*, a Commentary on Ṣaḥīḥ al-Bukhārī, on the commentary to Ḥadīth 6678 (al-Bukhārī, *al-Jāmi' aṣ-Ṣaḥiḥ*, *Kitāb al-Aymān wa'n-Nudhūr*, Ḥadīth 6678).

Al-Khaṭṭābī said: "Some of [the scholars] have presumed that – according to what has been revealed in the saying of Allāh ﷻ:

فَإِمَّا مَنًّا بَعْدُ وَإِمَّا فِدَآءً

Then, either showing grace after that, or ransom… [46]

showing grace to prisoners was specifically for the Prophet ﷺ but not for others."

[Ends Chapter 3.]

46. Holy Qur'ān, Sūrah Muḥammad (47), Verse 4.

CHAPTER

4

On what the Beloved Prophet Muḥammad ﷺ is specified with regarding honours and merits.

[The Life and Property of Prophet Muḥammad ﷺ]

He ﷺ is specified:

» with the rank of blessings

» that he ﷺ is not inherited. This was the same [ruling] for the [other] Prophets عليهم السلام, but they may bequeath all of their property in charity

» that his ﷺ property remains in his ﷺ ownership after his ﷺ [apparent] demise – it may be spent on his ﷺ family – according to one of two opinions, which Imām al-Ḥaramayn has acknowledged [though an-Nawawī has said that it leaves his ﷺ ownership and is spent in charity on the Muslims (*Fatḥ al-Qarīb*)]

» that if a villain intends [ill-will] against him ﷺ, it is obligatory upon whoever is present with him ﷺ to sacrifice his own life for his ﷺ sake. This has been related by a group of Companions رضي الله عنهم in *Zawā'id ar-Rawḍah*.

[His ﷺ Partaking in Battle]

Qatādah رحمه الله said: "It is from among his ﷺ unique particulars that if he ﷺ himself took part in battle, it is obliged on everyone to go with him ﷺ, based upon the saying of Allāh تعالى:

مَا كَانَ لِأَهْلِ ٱلْمَدِينَةِ وَمَنْ حَوْلَهُم مِّنَ ٱلْأَعْرَابِ
أَن يَتَخَلَّفُوا۟ عَن رَّسُولِ ٱللَّهِ

It is not permitted for the people of Madīnah and those wandering Arabs (living in the vicinities) around them to stay behind the Messenger of Allāh ﷺ.[47]

This ruling does not continue for anyone else among the Caliphs."

Ends [Qatādah's statement].

When he ﷺ is present within the row [in battle], it is forbidden on those with him ﷺ to turn their backs to him ﷺ lest they should face defeat or even abandon him ﷺ. Qatādah and al-Ḥasan said this.

They also said after him ﷺ [i.e. after his ﷺ era]: "To flee from an onslaught is not a major sin."

During his ﷺ era, Jihād was a personal obligation (*farḍ 'ayn*) – according to one of two opinions with us, but after him ﷺ it is among the acts that are a communal obligation (*farḍ kifāyah*).

47. Holy Qur'ān, Sūrat at-Tawbah (9), Verse 120.

[Laws for His ﷺ Daughters and Wives]

In some of the *Collections* of at-Tikrītī, I saw that *mahr al-mithl* (the customary and reasonable amount of dowry that a woman of her status would receive) cannot even be conceived for the daughter of the Prophet ﷺ as there was none of her status.

It is forbidden to look at the person of his ﷺ wives in cloaks – as al-Qāḍī 'Iyāḍ and others have explicitly mentioned.

The exposure of their faces, their hands – for witnessing or otherwise, directly asking questions from them and their praying in the open area of houses [are also prohibited].

Ma'mar said: "If his ﷺ wives nurse someone of majority age, he may come to them. This is specific to them. It is not permitted for all the rest of the people, except for what takes place at young age."

Ṭā'ūs said: "They had a known number of draws [for nursing], and the rest of the women also have known number of draws [for nursing] – it has been related that for them are ten draws and for other women are five draws."

They are Mothers of the Believers.

It is obligatory for them to stay at home after him ﷺ, as it is forbidden for them to go out, even if that be for Ḥajj or 'Umrah – according to one of two opinions.

It is permitted for them and for their children to remain inside the masjid while menstruating or being major ritually impure. That is how the texts are of the Mālikī [scholars].

[His ﷺ Ritual Prayer]

The supererogatory ritual prayer of the Prophet ﷺ while sitting is like his ﷺ standing, and his ﷺ act is additional for him ﷺ.

The worshippers address him ﷺ [in ritual prayer] with the words:

اَلسَّلَامُ عَلَيْكَ أَيُّهَا النَّبِيُّ

Peace be on you, O Prophet

but they do not address anyone else.

It is obligatory on anyone whom he ﷺ calls, who may be in ritual prayer, to respond to him ﷺ, and his ritual prayer will not be invalidated. This is the same [ruling] for the [other] Prophets عليهم السلام.

Whoever speaks while he ﷺ is delivering the [Jumu'ah prayer] sermon, his Jumu'ah prayer stands void.

It is obligatory to listen to his ﷺ recitation and internalise it when he ﷺ recites in an audible ritual prayer and when the Revelation is being delivered.

With regards to the saying of Allāh ﷻ:

إِذَا قِيلَ لَكُمْ تَفَسَّحُوا۟ فِى ٱلْمَجَـٰلِسِ فَٱفْسَحُوا۟

When it is said to you, "Make room in assemblies," then make room[48]

Mujāhid said: "It is specifically the assembly of the Prophet ﷺ."

Jābir ibn 'Abdullāh رضي الله عنه said:

لَيْسَ عَلَى مَنْ ضَحِكَ فِي الصَّلَاةِ إِعَادَةُ وُضُوءٍ , إِنَّمَا كَانَ ذَلِكَ لَهُمْ حِينَ ضَحِكُوا خَلْفَ رَسُولِ اللهِ صَلَّى اللهُ عَلَيْهِ وَسَلَّمَ

Anyone who laughs in ritual prayer need not renew wuḍū' – this [ruling] was for those who laughed behind the Messenger of Allāh ﷺ."[49]

[His ﷺ Marriage is Worship]

For him ﷺ, marriage is purely worship, as as-Subkī has said. According to us, it is not worship for anyone else, but rather it is among permitted acts, and worship is opposite to it.

[Attributing Wrongs to Him ﷺ]

Attributing a lie to him ﷺ is a major sin, quite unlike attributing a lie to anyone else. Al-Juwaynī said: "It is apostasy."

Whoever attributes a lie to him ﷺ, never ever shall his transmission [of reports] be accepted, even though he may repent – according to what many groups of Ḥadīth scholars have mentioned.

48. Holy Qur'ān, Sūrat al-Mujādilah (58), Verse 11.
49. Ad-Dāraquṭnī, *Kitāb aṭ-Ṭahārah*.

[Cautions to Others for Him ﷺ]

It is prohibited to:

i. walk in front of him ﷺ
ii. raise the voice over his ﷺ voice
iii. speak to him ﷺ in a loud voice
iv. call to him ﷺ from outside the room
v. shout to him ﷺ from afar
vii. call him ﷺ '*abū-nā* – our father' – according to one of two opinions
viii. say to him, '*rāʿi-nā* – have regard for us'.

[His ﷺ Purity]

[He is specified with:]

» his ﷺ urine and faeces being pure
» all his excreta are [pure and] drinkable – cures are sought therewith.

There is no doubt in the purity of his ﷺ hair; there is a difference with regards to [the hair of] others. He ﷺ distributed his ﷺ own hair among his ﷺ Companions رضي الله عنهم.

[His ﷺ Privileged Status]

[Furthermore, he ﷺ is specified with:]

» being free of all sins, be they minor or out of forgetfulness. This is the same [ruling] for the [other] Prophets عليهم السلام
» he ﷺ is free of doing what is disapproved
» loving him ﷺ is obligatory
» loving his ﷺ household رضي الله عنهم and his ﷺ Companions رضي الله عنهم is incumbent.

[Insulting Him ﷺ]

[Furthermore:]

» whoever slights him ﷺ has disbelieved (i.e. is not Muslim). It is said: "… or commits unlawful sexual intercourse (*zinā*) in his ﷺ presence."
» whoever wills his ﷺ death has disbelieved. This is the same [ruling] for the [other] Prophets عليهم السلام. Al-Maḥāmilī mentioned this in *al-Awsaṭ*
» inheriting them عليهم السلام has been declared unlawful on this basis, lest their heirs should wish for their death and thus become disbelievers.

Someone else said: "This is why his ﷺ hair did not turn white; women detest old age, and had this [detesting] taken place with them [i.e. the women], they would have become disbelievers. Thus, he ﷺ was protected from old age out of lenity to them."

[Furthermore:]

» one who insults him ﷺ is to be slain. This is the same [ruling] for the [other] Prophets ؑ

» insulting him ﷺ by euphemism is like insulting someone else explicitly

Ar-Rāfi'ī related this from al-Imām. An-Nawawī said: "There is no difference of opinion in this."

» no wife of any Prophet ؑ ever transgressed.

Al-Ḥasan said: "If the wife of the Prophet ﷺ commits unlawful sexual intercourse, she will not be pardoned."

[Insulting His ﷺ Wives and Companions ؓ]

Anyone who wrongfully accuses the wives of the Prophet ﷺ of unlawful sexual intercourse (*zinā*) his repentance shall never be accepted – according to what Ibn 'Abbās ؓ and others have said. He shall be slain – according to what al-Qāḍī 'Iyāḍ has related.

According to another saying: "Slaying is specific for one who insults 'Ā'ishah ؓ, while a double Hadd punishment is imposed for [insulting] the other wives." This is the same [ruling] for someone who insults the mother of any of the Companions ؓ.

Some of the Mālikī [scholars] have opined that whoever insults his ﷺ Companions ؓ is to be slain.

In *al-Muqni'*, Ibn Qudāmah said: "Whoever insults the mother of the Prophet ﷺ is to be slain, irrespective of whether he is a Muslim or a non-Muslim."

[Causing Distress to His ﷺ Daughters]

The children of his ﷺ daughters are ascribed to him ﷺ. It is also said: "… and also the children of the daughters of his ﷺ daughters." [It is mentioned] in a ḥadīth:

إِنَّ اللهَ لَمْ يَبْعَثْ نَبِيًّا قَطُّ إِلَّا جَعَلَ ذُرِّيَّتَهُ مِنْ صُلْبِهِ، غَيْرِيْ،
فَإِنَّ اللهَ جَعَلَ ذُرِّيَّتِيْ مِنْ صُلْبِ عَلِيٍّ

Verily, Allāh ﷻ never sends a Prophet ﷺ but that He ﷻ places his ﷺ descendants in his ﷺ loins, except for me; verily, Allāh ﷻ has placed my descendants in the loins of ʿAlī ﷺ.[50]

One may not marry while being married to [any of] his ﷺ daughters.

Al-Muḥibb aṭ-Ṭabarī has mentioned something finer than this. It is the ḥadīth of al-Miswar ibn Makhramah, when Ḥasan ibn Ḥasan proposed to marry [his daughter], he excused by saying:

فَاطِمَةُ بِضْعَةٌ مِنِّيْ يَقْبِضُنِيْ مَا يَقْبِضُهَا وَيَبْسُطُنِيْ مَا يَبْسُطُهَا

Fāṭimah is a piece of my flesh; distresses me whatever distresses her, and delights me whatever delights her.[51]

He said: "You have her daughter [as your wife]. If I was to marry [my daughter] to you, it would displease her [i.e. the daughter of Fāṭimah ﷺ]."

Thereafter, he said: "Therein is the evidence that the dead must be considered just as the living are considered."

He said: "In the *Commentary on at-Talkhīṣ*, Shaykh Abū ʿAlī as-Sinjī said: 'It is forbidden to marry again while being married to [any of] the daughters of the Prophet ﷺ. It may be that this refers to those who are connected to him ﷺ by prophethood. It is this that is a proof for [the aforementioned story].'"

Ends [Al-Muḥibb aṭ-Ṭabarī's statement].

If this [statement] was taken on its general basis, then it would entail it being forbidden to marry another woman while being married to the daughters among his ﷺ descendants, howsoever low, until the Day of Judgement. This is a [legally] suspended statement.

Whoever is related to him ﷺ by marriage through either of the two paths will not enter Hell.

---

50. Al-Khaṭīb; aṭ-Ṭabarānī.
51. Al-Ḥākim, *al-Mustadrak*.

[Miscellaneous Issues Pertaining to His ﷺ Unique Status]

With regards to [the authenticity of] the prayer-niche (*miḥrāb*) of the Prophet ﷺ towards which he ﷺ prayed, it will not be investigated – neither to the left of it and nor to the right of it

» the Prayer in the state of Fear (*ṣalāt al-khawf*) is specific to his ﷺ era – according to the saying of Abū Yūsuf and al-Muzanī, because there is no alternative to his ﷺ leadership, as opposed to [the leadership of] other [Prophets ﷺ]
» his ﷺ rank is elevated with supplications of mercy made for him ﷺ – according to what a group [of scholars] have mentioned
» it is forbidden to manufacture a seal according to the seal of his ﷺ ring. No one is permitted to make a seal upon ' محمد رسول الله – *Muḥammadu'r-Rasūlu'Llāh* (Muḥammad is the Messenger of Allāh ﷺ)'
» he ﷺ does not speak of his ﷺ own desire
» in anger and when pleased, he ﷺ says nothing but the Truth
» his ﷺ dreams are Revelation. This is the same [ruling] for the [other] Prophets ﷺ
» insanity and long periods of chronic unconsciousness are not possible for the Prophets ﷺ – according to what Shaykh Abū Ḥāmid has mentioned in his *at-Ta'līq*, and al-Bulqīnī has acknowledged in *Ḥawāshī ar-Rawḍah.*

As-Subkī has cautioned that the unconsciousness of the Prophets ﷺ is unlike the unconsciousness of other people, just as their sleeping is unlike the sleeping of other people.

Visual impairment is not possible for them – according to what as-Subkī has mentioned.

[Prophets ﷺ are Free of Blemishes]

Regarding the claim of the Banū Isrā'īl that Prophet Mūsā ﷺ was 'heavy of tongue and mouth,' and Allāh ﷻ cured him ﷺ, al-Qāḍī 'Iyāḍ said: "The Prophets ﷺ are free from blemishes in their created form and manners; fit regarding physical disabilities and imperfections; [free from] any inclination towards anything [mentioned] in some [books of] history that attribute defects to some of them ﷺ. In fact, Allāh ﷻ has rendered them ﷺ free of all blemishes, and all shortcomings that cause debasement or disliking in the hearts [of people]."

[His ﷺ Issuing Specific Commands]

He ﷺ specifies whom he ﷺ wills with [legal] commands, such as rating the witnessing of Khuzaymah ؓ equal to the witnessing of two men.

[Furthermore,] his ﷺ permitting:

» Sālim ؓ to be nursed, though he ؓ was of majority age
» wailing for that woman – Khawlah bint Ḥakīm ؓ
» hastening the payment of two years' charity for ʿAbbās ؓ
» omitting the mourning for Asmāʾ bint ʿUmays ؓ
» combining his ﷺ own name and filial appellation for any child born to ʿAlī ؓ
» remaining inside the masjid in the state of major ritual impurity for ʿAlī ؓ
» opening the door of the house [of ʿAlī ؓ] into the masjid
» opening the window into [the masjid] for Abū Bakr ؓ
» eating of his own atonement – for the one who had invalidated his fast with sexual relations in Ramaḍān
» sacrificing a she-kid (*ʿanāq*) – for Abū Burdah ibn Niyār ؓ
» diversion [to sacrifice a six month old kid] – for ʿUqbah ibn ʿĀmir ؓ and Zayd ibn Khālid ؓ
» marriage – for that man ؓ to give what he possesses from the Qurʾān [as dowry] – according to what a group [of scholars] have mentioned, as well as a *mursal* (expedited) ḥadīth being reported in this regard. Makḥūl said: "This is not permitted for anyone after the Prophet ﷺ."

[Furthermore, his ﷺ permitting:]

» wearing silk for az-Zubayr ؓ and ʿAbdurraḥmān ibn ʿAwf ؓ – according to what a group [of scholars] have said, and it is our opinion also
» wearing a gold ring – for al-Barāʾ ibn ʿĀzib ؓ
» stipulating clientage (*walāʾ*) for ʿĀʾishah ؓ with regards to the manumission of Barīrah ؓ. This is not valid – according to what some of [the scholars] have stated
» the [seeing of] nudeness by Thaʿlabah ibn Yazīd al-Ḥārithī ؓ and [consequently] his ؓ becoming withered – according to what al-Wāqidī has opined
» option [to conclude or revoke a purchase] regarding unfairness to Ḥabbān ibn Munqidh ؓ – according to what an-Nawawī has mentioned in the *Commentary on Muslim*

» leaving the state of *Iḥrām* because of illness, for Ḍubā'ah bint az-Zubayr 🕮 – according to one of two opinions

» omitting to spend the night at Minā for the Banū 'Abbās 🕮 – because they gave water [to the pilgrims], according to one opinion – the Banū Hāshim, according to another [opinion]

» offering two units of ritual prayer after '*aṣr* [prayer] for 'Ā'ishah 🕮

» acceptance of gifts for Mu'ādh ibn Jabal 🕮 when he 🕮 dispatched him 🕮 to Yemen.

It is mentioned in *al-Mustadrak* and others, as reported by Anas 🕮, that Umm Sulaym 🕮 married Abū Talḥah 🕮 on the condition of him 🕮 becoming Muslim. Thābit said: "I have never heard of any woman whose dowry may have been nobler than that of Umm Sulaym's – and that is to become Muslim."

[Furthermore:]

» he 🕮 returned the wife of Abū Rukānah 🕮 to him 🕮 without the process of legalisation of remarriage (*ḥalālah*) after he 🕮 had divorced her thrice

» a man became Muslim on the condition that he would not perform ritual prayer except two units, and he 🕮 accepted it from him

» he 🕮 fired an arrow for 'Uthmān 🕮 in [the Battle of] Badr. He 🕮 did not fire [any arrow] for anyone who was absent other than for him 🕮. Abū Dāwūd reported it from Ibn 'Umar 🕮.

Al-Khaṭṭābī said: "This is specific for 'Uthmān 🕮, as he 🕮 was taking care of the ill daughter of the Messenger of Allāh 🕮."

[Furthermore:]

» he 🕮 formed the brotherhood among his 🕮 Companions 🕮 and established heirdom between them 🕮. This was not permitted for anyone else. Ibn Zayd said this

» he 🕮 specified the wives of the Migrants [from Makkah to Madīnah] to inherit rather than their husbands as they were foreigners [in Madīnah] and had no refuge

» Anas 🕮 would fast from the rising of the sun rather than from the rising of the dawn. It is obvious that this was specific to him 🕮

» the infants of his 🕮 Prophetic Household (*Ahl al-Bayt*) would fast when they were breastfeeding

» it was forbidden for the Companions ﷺ to leave until they had sought his ﷺ permission after they ﷺ had assembled with him ﷺ for a collective affair they ﷺ would say to him ﷺ:

بِأَبِي أَنْتَ وَأُمِّي

My father and mother be devoted to you (O Messenger of Allāh ﷺ)

according to what some [scholars] have stated, this is not permitted [to be said] to anyone else.

[His ﷺ Natural Disposition]

[He ﷺ is specified in that:]

» he ﷺ would see behind him ﷺ as he ﷺ would see in front of him ﷺ
» Razīn added: "… and to his ﷺ right and his ﷺ left."
» he ﷺ would see at night and in darkness as he ﷺ would see during the day and in the light
» his ﷺ saliva would sweeten salty water and suffice the suckling
» his ﷺ armpits were white, not changing colour and nor with any hair
» his ﷺ voice and hearing could reach that which nothing else could reach
» his ﷺ eye would sleep but his ﷺ heart would not sleep
» he ﷺ never yawned
» he ﷺ never had a nocturnal emission. This is the same [case] for the [other] Prophets ﷺ – as is stated in the Three Books
» his ﷺ sweat was sweeter than musk
» when he ﷺ walked with a tall man, he ﷺ would be taller than him
» when he ﷺ sat, his ﷺ shoulders would be higher than all of those seated
» his ﷺ shadow did not fall on the ground
» no shadow of his ﷺ was seen in the sunlight or moonlight. Ibn Sab' said: "… that is because he ﷺ was light (*nūr*)." Razīn said: "… out of the overpowering of his ﷺ lights."

[Furthermore:]

» no fly ever sat on his ﷺ clothing
» no louse ever harmed him ﷺ
» when he ﷺ mounted an animal, it would neither dung nor urinate while he ﷺ was mounted upon it. Ibn Isḥāq related this. Upon this, some historians have based his ﷺ circumambulating the Ka'bah while mounted upon his

camel, and thus they rendered it among his ﷺ unique particulars. This is not permitted for anyone else

- his ﷺ countenance was as if the sun shone through it
- his ﷺ foot did not have a hollow in its middle
- his ﷺ small toe was apparent
- when he ﷺ walked, the earth would fold up before him ﷺ
- he ﷺ was given the strength of forty [men] in sexual relations and in grasping. According to the narration of Muqātil, he ﷺ was given the strength of more than seventy [men]. According to Mujāhid: "He ﷺ was given the strength of more than forty men – each man being from among the inhabitants of Paradise." The strength of a man from the inhabitants of Paradise is akin to a hundred from those of this world, and thus, he ﷺ was given the strength of four thousand [men]. By this is removed the ambiguity that some of [the scholars] had when they said: "How was he ﷺ given the strength of only forty [men] when Prophet Sulaymān ﷷ was given the strength of a hundred men – or a thousand men, according to what has also been reported?" It was a much-needed duty to respond to this. It has been reported via many chains:

أَتَانِي جِبْرِيْلُ بِقِدْرٍ فَأَكَلْتُ مِنْهَا فَأُعْطِيْتُ قُوَّةَ أَرْبَعِيْنَ رَجُلاً فِي الْجِمَاعِ

Jibrīl brought me a pot from which I ate and was given the strength of forty men.[52]

In other words:

مَا أُرِيْدُ أَنْ آتِيَ النِّسَاءَ سَاعَةً إِلَّا فَعَلْتُ

If I want I may visit [my] wives at any moment.[53]

In *Sirāj al-Murīdīn*, al-Qāḍī Abū Bakr ibn al-ʿArabī said: "Allāh ﷻ has bestowed upon His ﷻ Messenger ﷺ a magnificent quality, and that is the meagreness of eating and yet having the power to have sexual relations."

[Furthermore:]

- he ﷺ was the most content of people in terms of food – even one morsel would suffice him ﷺ, and one morsel and one mouthful would quench his ﷺ thirst

52. Ibn Saʿd, *aṭ-Ṭabaqāt al-Kubrā*.
53. Ibn Saʿd, *aṭ-Ṭabaqāt al-Kubrā*; *Kanz al-ʿUmmāl*.

» he ﷺ was the strongest of people in terms of sexual relations
» the traces of excreta from him ﷺ were never seen. In fact, the ground would swallow them and the fragrance of musk would be sensed at their location. This is the same [case] for the [other] Prophets ﷺ.

[His ﷺ Noble Birth]

[It is from among his ﷺ unique particulars that:]

» there has never been anyone indecent among his ﷺ ancestors ever since Prophet Ādam ﷺ
» he ﷺ has passed [down through the loins] from those who prostrate [to Allāh ﷻ] until he ﷺ appeared as a Prophet ﷺ
» there has never been a group except that he ﷺ was among the best of them
» his ﷺ parents did not bear anyone but him ﷺ
» the idols fell over when he ﷺ was born
» he ﷺ was born circumcised, with his ﷺ umbilical cord cut, and clean without any dirt
» he ﷺ went to the ground in prostration with his ﷺ [right index] finger raised as if earnestly supplicating
» at his ﷺ birth, his ﷺ mother ﷺ saw a light emit from her ﷺ whereby the palaces of ash-Shām (the Levant) were illuminated. This is similar to what the mothers of the [other] Prophets ﷺ saw
» some [scholars] said: "No woman every nursed him ﷺ except that she became Muslim." They said: "He ﷺ had four wet-nurses:

i. his ﷺ mother ﷺ – her ﷺ being given life and becoming Muslim is mentioned in a ḥadīth[54],
ii. Ḥalīmah as-Sa'diyah ﷺ,
iii. Thuwaybah ﷺ, and
iv. Umm Ayman ﷺ."

Ends [their statement].

54. Al-Bajūrī, *Jawharat at-Tawḥīd'* ; al-Khaṭīb al-Baghdādī, *as-Sābiq wa'l-Lāḥiq*; as-Suyūṭī, *al-Ḥāwī li'l-Fatāwī'*.

[His ﷺ Childhood]

[It is also from among his ﷺ unique particulars that:]

» his ﷺ cradle would rock because of the angels' rocking [it]. Ibn Sab' has mentioned this

» the moon would talk to him ﷺ tenderly when he ﷺ was in his ﷺ cradle, and it would move about as he ﷺ pointed to it

» he ﷺ would speak in his ﷺ cradle

» clouds would shade him ﷺ when it was hot.

[His ﷺ Physical Miracles]

[Furthermore:]

» the shade of trees would incline towards him ﷺ whenever he ﷺ went to it

» he ﷺ would spend the night in hunger but would wake up sated as his ﷺ Lord ﷻ would feed him ﷺ and give him ﷺ to drink from [the food and drink of] Paradise

» he ﷺ would become ill equal to two men becoming ill – for receiving double the reward

» he ﷺ is free of all effective defects. Al-Quḍā'ī mentioned this in his *at-Ta'rīkh'*.

[His ﷺ Noble Soul being Taken and His ﷺ Funeral]

[It is from among his ﷺ unique particulars that:]

» his ﷺ soul was returned to him ﷺ after it was taken

» thereafter, he ﷺ was given the choice whether to remain in this world or return to Allāh ﷻ – he ﷺ preferred to be returned to Him ﷻ. This is the same [case] for the [other] Prophets ﷩

» during his ﷺ terminal illness, his ﷺ Lord ﷻ sent [Angel] Jibrīl ﷺ to him ﷺ for three days, asking him ﷺ his ﷺ condition

» when the Angel of Death ﷺ came to him ﷺ, an angel called Ismā'īl ﷺ also descended with him ﷺ. He ﷺ lives in the atmosphere, never having climbed to the sky nor having come down to the earth prior to that day

» the voice of the Angel of Death ﷺ was heard crying over it [i.e. the taking of the soul of Prophet Muḥammad ﷺ], proclaiming (in a sorrowful lamenting manner):

- his ﷺ Lord ﷻ sent blessings on him ﷺ, as well as the angels
- in groups, the people prayed over him ﷺ, without an imām (leader of the ritual prayer congregation). They said: "He ﷺ is your (i.e. our) leader, in [physical] life and in [apparent] death." [They prayed] without any well-known funeral supplication
- the ritual prayer [for the funeral] was repeated over him ﷺ until the men had finished, followed by the women and then the children
- other than for him ﷺ, it [i.e. the ritual funeral prayer] is not repeated for anyone – according to Mālik and Abū Ḥanīfah
- according to one group [of scholars], it is from among his ﷺ unique particulars that he ﷺ was not conventionally prayed over, as the people were entering in groups, supplicating and leaving. This has been reasoned as being due to his ﷺ merit that he ﷺ was not in need of it [i.e. the ritual funeral prayer]
- he ﷺ was left without burial (i.e. he ﷺ lay in state) for three days
- he ﷺ was buried during the night. This is disapproved for others – according to al-Ḥasan, and unorthodox – according to all the [other] scholars
- he ﷺ was buried inside his ﷺ room where he ﷺ passed away. This is the same [case] for the [other] Prophets عليهم السلام. It is more excellent for others to be buried in the cemetery
- velour was laid out in his ﷺ grave-niche.

Both [aforementioned] acts are disapproved for us. Wakīʿ said: "This is something specific for the Prophet ﷺ and disapproved for anyone other than him ﷺ, as an agreement between the Ḥanafī [scholars] and the Mālikī [scholars]."

It is also among his ﷺ unique particulars that:

- he ﷺ was bathed [for his ﷺ funeral] in his ﷺ shirt. They say: "This is disapproved for anyone else."
- upon his ﷺ death, the earth was made to go dark.

[His ﷺ Grave]

[It is from among his ﷺ unique particulars that:]

- he ﷺ is not squeezed in his ﷺ grave. This is the same [case] for the [other] Prophets عليهم السلام. [Even though,] besides these, no righteous person or anyone else is safe from the squeezing. [It is mentioned] in the *at-Tadhkirah* of al-Qurṭubī: "… except for Fāṭimah bint Asad – due to blessings from him ﷺ."
- it is prohibited to offer ritual prayer over his ﷺ grave and to make it a place of prostration
- Al-Adhruʿī said: "It is prohibited to urinate near the graves of Prophets عليهم السلام, and it is disapproved near the graves of others."
- his ﷺ body does not decay. This is the same [case] for the [other] Prophets عليهم السلام
- the earth does not eat their عليهم السلام flesh, and neither do predatory animals
- there is no doubt in their bodies being [ritually] pure, though there is a difference of opinion regarding [the bodies of] others
- no [inheritable] endowment continues to their children that some [people] have for others
- it is not permitted for the coerced to eat the body of any Prophet عليه السلام, as he عليه السلام is alive in his عليه السلام grave, wherein he عليه السلام offers ritual prayer with an *adhān* and an *iqāmah*. This is the same [case] for the [all the] Prophets عليهم السلام. It is thus said: "There is no waiting period (*ʿiddah*) due on his ﷺ wives."
- an angel عليه السلام is appointed at his ﷺ grave who delivers the blessings of those who send blessings to him ﷺ, and he presents the deeds of his ﷺ Community to him ﷺ, and thus, he ﷺ seeks pardon for them
- the calamity of his ﷺ [apparent] death is general for his ﷺ Community until the Day of Judgement
- it is permitted to sacrifice [an animal] on his ﷺ behalf after his [apparent] demise – according to what al-Bulqīnī has mentioned.

[Seeing Him ﷺ in a Dream]

[It is from among his ﷺ unique particulars that:]

- whoever sees him ﷺ in his dream has seen him ﷺ in reality, for Shayṭān cannot imitate his ﷺ appearance
- to whomever he ﷺ issues a command in a dream, it is incumbent on him to fulfil it – according to one of two opinions. The other opinion [says:] "… it is recommended"

- it is narrated that the first things that will be removed are: seeing him ﷺ in a dream, the Qur'ān and the Black Stone (*al-Ḥajar al-Aswad*).

[His ﷺ Blessed Name and His ﷺ Noble Traditions]

[It is from among his ﷺ unique particulars that:]

- reading of his ﷺ ḥadīths is [an act of] worship for which reward is given, just like recitation of the Qur'ān – according to one of two reports
- ire does not devour anything that his face [or hand] has touched. This is the same [case] for the [other] Prophets ﷺ
- anything given his ﷺ name is auspicious, and profitable in this world and the Hereafter
- it is disapproved to carry into the lavatory anything with his ﷺ name written on it
- it is recommended to bathe for reading his ﷺ ḥadīth and to wear perfume
- voices are not to be raised [where a ḥadīth is being read]
- it is read in lofty places
- it is disapproved for the one who is reading it to stand for anyone
- those who carry it, their countenances shall remain ever fresh, based upon the saying of the Prophet ﷺ:

نَضَّرَ اللّٰهُ امْرَءًا سَمِعَ مَقَالَتِي فَوَعَاهَا فَأَدَّاهَا كَمَا سَمِعَهَا

Allāh ﷻ keep a person fresh who hears my saying and retains it,
and then he transmits it as he heard it[55]

among all the [various kinds of] scholars, they have been specified with titles [such as]; *ḥāfiẓ* (retainer), *amīr al-mu'minīn* (leader of the Believers).

- books of ḥadīth are placed upon racks, like the Qur'ān.

[His ﷺ Noble Companions ﷺ]

Companionship is established for someone who associates with him ﷺ [even] for a moment, as opposed to a Successor with a Companion; it is not established except with a lengthy duration of company with him – according to the more correct opinion among the theoreticians. The difference is due to the tremendousness of the prophetic status and of its lights.

55. Aṭ-Ṭabarānī, *al-Mu'jam al-Awsaṭ*, etc.

[Furthermore:]
» the mere falling of his ﷺ vision on an unmannerly bedouin makes him speak with wisdom.
» all of his ﷺ Companions ﷺ are morally upright
» the moral uprightness of any one of them ﷺ is not investigated, unlike all the [other] reporters [of ḥadīth]
» they ﷺ do not become morally corrupt by pursuing that with which others become morally corrupt – as he [i.e. Jalāluddīn as-Suyūṭī] has mentioned in *Sharḥ Jam' al-Jawāmi'*.

Muḥammad ibn Ka'b al-Quraẓī said: "Allāh ﷻ has determined Paradise and [His ﷻ] pleasure for all the Companions ﷺ in His ﷻ Book, for the good among them and the sinful, and He ﷻ has stipulated for those after them ﷺ to follow them ﷺ in good faith."

[His ﷺ Grave and His ﷺ Masjid]

[It is from among his ﷺ unique particulars that:]
» it is not disapproved for women to visit his ﷺ grave, unlike it being disapproved for them [to visit any of the] other graves. Rather, it is recommended, as al-'Irāqī said in his *Nukat* that there was no doubt about it
» the worshipper in his ﷺ masjid is not to spit to his left [if he at all must] – though it is a practice in all the [other] masjids
» even if his ﷺ masjid was built towards Sana'a (in Yemen), it would still be his ﷺ masjid
» no door, window or skylight may be opened into it.

[Sending Blessings Upon Him ﷺ]

[Furthermore:]
» at the lips of every human are two angels who do not preserve [anything] but the blessings sent specifically upon him ﷺ.

[Furthermore,] among his ﷺ unique particulars is:
» the obligation of sending blessings upon him ﷺ in the [position of] *tashahhud* (sitting and reciting the testimony in ritual prayer) – according to us. This is enumerated in *al-Khādim*, extracted from *al-Ḥalabiyyāt* of as-Subkī

- [the obligation of sending blessings upon him ﷺ] whenever he ﷺ is mentioned – according to al-Ḥalīmī and aṭ-Ṭaḥāwī, as this is not less [important] than responding with a supplication for the sneezer. Al-Qāḍī Tājuddīn as-Subkī, from among the later [scholars], has preferred this opinion
- one who sends blessings upon him ﷺ at a point of indecency or mockery, or renders blessings upon him ﷺ that suffice to abuse another – he becomes non-Muslim. Al-Ḥalīmī mentioned this and it was transmitted in *al-Khādim.*

[Accept All His ﷺ Decisions]

[Furthermore:]

- if he ﷺ makes a decision against someone and that person has a concern in his heart regarding his ﷺ decision against him, he becomes non-Muslim, as opposed to other decision-makers. Al-Iṣṭakhrī mentioned this in *Ādāb al-Qaḍā.*

[Only One Imām After Him ﷺ]

[Furthermore,] among his ﷺ unique particulars is:

- that there will be only one imām after him ﷺ – this was not the case for the Prophets ﷺ prior to him ﷺ. Ibn Surāqah said this in *al-A'dād.*

[His ﷺ Noble Family ﷺ]

[Furthermore, among his ﷺ unique particulars is:]

- [his ﷺ] permission to bequeath absolutely to his ﷺ family – as for others there is an opinion that it is not permitted due to an obscurity in the wording, and due to it vacillating between close relatives and loans. They [i.e. the scholars] mentioned this in *Bāb al-Waṣiyyah* (Chapters on Wills and Bequests)
- there is none suitable in marriage to his ﷺ descendants – they [i.e. the scholars] mentioned this in *Bāb an-Nikāḥ* (Chapters on Marriage)
- [the title] *ashrāf* is applied to them; the singular is *sharīf* – and they are the children of 'Alī ﷺ, 'Aqīl ﷺ, Ja'far ﷺ, and 'Abbās ﷺ. This is the nomenclature of the earlier generations

» in Egypt, the specification of [the word] *sharīf* was to the children of al-Ḥasan ⬥ and al-Ḥusayn ⬥, especially during the era of the Fāṭimīs (Fatimids) Caliphs.

[His ⬥ Daughter Fāṭimah ⬥]

The author of *al-Fatāwā az-Ẓahīriyyah*, from among the Ḥanafī [scholars] has mentioned: "Verily, it is from among his ⬥ unique particulars that his daughter Fāṭimah ⬥ did not experience menses; whenever she gave birth, she would become pure from her postpartum bleeding after a moment, so that she would not miss a ritual prayer." He said: "... and that is why she ⬥ is called '*az-Ẓahrā* – bright-faced'."

One of our companions, [namely] al-Muḥibb aṭ-Ṭabarī has mentioned this in *Dhakha'ir al-'Uqbā*, and he has quoted a ḥadīth on it: "Verily, she has bright white eyes with intensely dark pupils, wheat-coloured skin; [she is] pure and purified; she does not experience menses, and nor does she have traces of bleeding during menstruation and nor childbirth."

In the *ad-Dalā'il* of al-Bayhaqī [it is mentioned]:

$$أَنَّهُ وَضَعَ يَدَهُ عَلَى صَدْرِهَا فَرَفَعَ عَنْهَا الْجُوْعَ فَمَا جَاعَتْ بَعْدُ$$

Verily, he ⬥ placed his ⬥ hand on her chest and removed hunger
from her – she never felt hungry after that

and [it is stated] in *al-Musnad* of Aḥmad, etc.: "... that when she ⬥ was close to death, she bathed herself and bequeathed no-one to reveal her. Thus, 'Alī ⬥ buried her with that bathing."

Imām 'Ilmuddīn al-'Irāqī has mentioned: "Verily, Fāṭimah ⬥ and her brother Ibrāhīm ⬥ are unanimously more excellent than the four [Rightly-Guided] Caliphs."

It has been narrated from Mālik that he said: "I do not hold anyone more excellent than the piece of flesh from the Prophet ⬥ (i.e. Fāṭimah ⬥)."

[His ⬥ Wife 'Ā'ishah ⬥]

In *Ma'ānī al-Āthār* of aṭ-Ṭaḥāwī, Abū Ḥanīfah said: "The people were non-marriageable relatives (*maḥram*) to 'Ā'ishah ⬥ – with whomever among them she travelled, she would be travelling with a non-marriageable relative."

The people are not like that (i.e. non-marriageable) to women other than her ⬥.

[His ﷺ Blessed Body Parts, etc.]

[It is] among his ﷺ unique particulars that Razīn has mentioned:

» "Some of his ﷺ hair fell into fire but did not burn
» he ﷺ wiped his ﷺ hand over the head of a bald man and his hair grew straight away
» he ﷺ placed his ﷺ hand on a sick person and he recovered immediately
» he ﷺ planted a palm-tree and it gave fruit that very year
» he ﷺ shook 'Umar ﷺ with his ﷺ hand and he ﷺ became Muslim immediately
» his ﷺ right index finger was the longest of his ﷺ fingers
» he ﷺ would not point towards anything except that it would follow him ﷺ
» he ﷺ would not tread on a stone except that he ﷺ would leave a trace upon it – or a palm-tree except that he ﷺ would leave some effect upon it
» whenever he ﷺ would smile at night, he ﷺ would brighten up the room
» he ﷺ would hear the swishing of [the Angel] Jibrīl's ﷺ wings when he ﷺ would be as far as the Furthest Lote-Tree (*Sidrat al-Muntahā*)
» he ﷺ would smell his ﷺ fragrance when he ﷺ would be concentrated in Revelation to him ﷺ
» a Muslim would touch his ﷺ body and the Fire [of Hell] would not affect him
» a group of Muslims would be gathered around him ﷺ [all the time]
» he ﷺ spoke little
» when instructed to fight in battle, he ﷺ would exert himself ﷺ
» it was prohibited for people to enter his ﷺ house without permission
» and [it was prohibited for them] to sit there for long."

Ends [Razīn's statement].

[His ﷺ Performing Funeral Prayers]

[It is mentioned] in *Nukat al-Ḥāwī* of an-Nāshirī: "It was reported from him ﷺ that he ﷺ did not pray [the funeral prayer] over his ﷺ son Ibrāhīm ﷺ."

Some scholars have said that this was because he ﷺ was needless [of it] due to the prophethood of his father ﷺ out of the proximity of blessings, just as a martyr (*shahīd*) is needless [of a funeral prayer (according to the Shāfi'ī school)] due to the proximity of martyrdom.

[It is mentioned] in *al-Mustadrak* on the authority of Anas ﷺ: "Verily, he ﷺ prayed [the funeral prayer] over Ḥamzah ﷺ but he ﷺ did not pray over any of the other martyrs."

[It is mentioned] in another ḥadīth that he ﷺ said the *takbīr* (Allāhu Akbar) seventy times over him ﷺ, and in another that he ﷺ prayed over him ﷺ seventy [funeral] prayers.

In the two Ṣaḥīḥs [of Imām al-Bukhārī and Imām Muslim – Allāh be pleased with them], etc., from the ḥadīth of 'Uqbah ibn 'Āmir ﷺ, that he ﷺ went out one day and prayed his prayer for the dead over the [martyrs] of Uḥud, and that was near to his ﷺ [apparent] demise, eight years after their death.[56]

[It is mentioned] in a *ṣaḥīḥ* (sound) narration that he ﷺ went out to the people [buried at] al-Baqī' [cemetery] and prayed over them.

Al-Qāḍī 'Iyāḍ said, concerning some of them: "It is taken for this to be the conventional ritual prayer made over the dead, and it would have been specific to his ﷺ family. It may also be that he ﷺ desired his ﷺ prayer to be general for them, as there may be among them those who were buried when he ﷺ was not there, or they were unknown and so he ﷺ had not prayed for them – thus, he ﷺ rendered his ﷺ blessings common to [all of] them."

[His ﷺ Legal Decisions]

[It is] among [his ﷺ] unique particulars that it is permitted say to the Prophet ﷺ: "Adjudicate as you ﷺ wish, because whatever you ﷺ decide is correct and agreed by me." Most [scholars] have acknowledged this in the principles [of religion]. It is due to the lowliness in his status that this not the case with any scholar – according to what as-Sam'ānī has preferred.

One group has gone [with the opinion] that it is among his ﷺ unique particulars: his ﷺ being prohibited to practise independent reasoning (*ijtihād*) due to his ﷺ having the capacity to reach certainty through Revelation. [This prohibition is] also for everyone else during his ﷺ era due to his being able to reach certainty by seeking it from him ﷺ.

[It is mentioned] in *Sharḥ al-Manār* of as-Sakākī: "The Revelation is a proof to whom it is given as well as to others – if to whom it is revealed is a Prophet ﷺ and he ﷺ knows that it is from Allāh ﷻ, but not if he is a Friend [of Allāh ﷻ] (*walī*)."

56. Al-Bukhārī, *al-Jāmi' aṣ-Ṣaḥīḥ*, *Kitāb al-Maghāzī*, Ḥadīth 4042. Similar ḥadīths are found in Muslim, *al-Musnad aṣ-Ṣaḥīḥ*, Abū Dāwūd, *as-Sunan*, ash-Shāfi'ī, *Kitāb al-Umm*, etc.

[It is mentioned] in *Tafsīr ibn al-Mundhir*, on the authority of 'Amr ibn Dīnār, that a man said to 'Umar ﷺ: "Adjudicate according to what Allāh ﷻ has shown to you." He ﷺ replied: "Quiet! This is something specific to the Prophet ﷺ."

[It is mentioned] in *Sunan Sa'īd ibn Manṣūr*, on the authority of Sa'īd ibn Jubayr who said: "We never heard of a Prophet ﷺ being slain in battle."

[It is mentioned] in al-Mabṣūṭ, from among the books of the Ḥanafī [scholars], on the authority of one of them: "Verily, endowment is binding specifically upon the Prophets ﷺ and not upon others." They have taken a ḥadīth for it:

لَا نُوْرَثُ ، مَا تَرَكْنَاهُ صَدَقَةٌ

We are not inherited; what we leave is charity.[57]

This proponent has rendered it exclusive to the saying of Abū Ḥanīfah: "Endowment is binding."

[His ﷺ Greeting Others]

[It is mentioned] in *Tafsīr Ibn al-Mundhir*, on the authority of Ibn Jurayj, that whenever they would enter upon the Prophet ﷺ, he ﷺ would begin by greeting them with peace – he ﷺ would say:

سَلَامٌ عَلَيْكُمْ

Peace be with you

It was the same whenever he ﷺ would meet any of them, due to the saying of Allāh ﷻ:

وَإِذَا جَآءَكَ ٱلَّذِينَ يُؤْمِنُونَ بِـَٔايَـٰتِنَا فَقُلْ سَلَـٰمٌ عَلَيْكُمْ

And when those who believe in Our Signs come to you (O Messenger ﷺ), then say (to them): Peace be with you.[58]

There are two unique particulars in this: his ﷺ initiating the greeting with peace to the one entering and to the passerby.

For us, it is a sunnah (Prophetic practice) that the one who enters and the passerby initiate [the greeting]. The incumbency of initiating for him ﷺ is due to the command [given] in the verse, whereas initiating [the greeting] is not incumbent on any person from [this] Community.

57. Al-Bukhārī, *al-Jāmi' aṣ-Ṣaḥīḥ*; ash-Shawkānī, *Nayl al-Awṭār*.
58. Holy Qur'ān, Sūrat al-An'ām (6), Verse 54.

[His ﷺ Having Beatific Vision]

It is from among his ﷺ unique particulars that seeing Allāh ﷻ in dreams is certainly possible for him ﷺ whereas it is not possible for anyone else – according to one of two opinions. This is preferential, and Abū Manṣūr al-Māturīdī is also of this opinion.

[His ﷺ Encompassing Language]

[It is mentioned] in *ar-Risālah* of Imām ash-Shāfi'ī:

لَا يُحِيطُ بِاللُّغَةِ إِلَّا نَبِيٌّ

None can encompass the language other than a Prophet ﷺ

[His ﷺ Manners]

There is a ḥadīth in *al-Mustadrak*:

لَيْسَ لِنَبِيٍّ أَن يَدْخُلَ بَيْتاً مُزَوَّقاً

It is not permitted for a Prophet ﷺ *to enter a decorated house*[59]

[A Prophet ﷺ Removing Hair]

Ibn 'Abbās رضي الله عنهما said: "No Prophet ﷺ ever applied paste for removing pubic hair (*nawrah*)."

[Dreams of Prophets عليهم السلام]

Qatādah رحمه الله said: "The interpretation of dreams is inconclusive. Allāh ﷻ renders any of them true and He ﷻ renders any of them false."

Ibn Jarīr said: "The [case] is not the same for non-Prophets. As for [the dreams of] Prophets ﷺ, the people have not interpreted as 'they unequivocally happen'."

59. Aḥmad, *al-Musnad*; Ibn Mājah, *as-Sunan*; Abū Dāwūd, *as-Sunan*; al-Ḥākim, *al-Mustadrak*, etc.

[Deceiving Him ﷺ]

Tha'labah ibn Ḥāṭib lied and thus, as a punishment to him, accepting [the payment of] *zakāh* from him was prohibited – Abū Bakr ؓ, 'Umar ؓ and 'Uthmān ؓ did not accept it from him ﷺ, until he died during his [i.e. 'Uthmān's ؓ] caliphate.

Tamīmah bint Wahb lied, and so he ﷺ forbade her being returned to her divorcing husband, [namely] Rifā'ah ؓ. [Afterwards, even] Abū Bakr ؓ and neither 'Umar ؓ returned her to him ؓ. 'Umar ؓ said to her: "If you come to me after this, I shall have stones pelted at you."

A man withheld some barley and then brought it to him ﷺ [after the collection and distribution], and he ﷺ said to him:

كفَّ، أَنْتَ تَجِيْئُ بِهِ يَوْمَ الْقِيَامَةِ فَلَنْ أَقْبَلَهُ عَنْكَ

Stop there! You will bring it on the Day of Judgement and
I shall not accept (it) from you.

Ibn 'Abbās ؓ said: "Everyone is held for what they say and then released, except for the Prophet [Muḥammad ﷺ]."

Ibn 'Abbās ؓ said, regarding the saying of Allāh ﷻ:

لَهُۥ مُعَقِّبَٰتٌ مِّنۢ بَيْنِ يَدَيْهِ وَمِنْ خَلْفِهِۦ يَحْفَظُونَهُۥ مِنْ أَمْرِ ٱللَّهِ

For him ﷺ, there are angels in front of him ﷺ and behind him ﷺ;
they protect him ﷺ by the command of Allāh ﷻ,[60]

"... this is specific to the Prophet ﷺ."

In the *Musnad ash-Shāfi'ī* is a ḥadīth:

نُصِرْتُ بِالصَّبَا وَ كَانَتْ عَذَاباً عَلَى مَنْ قَبْلِي

I have been given the support of the easterly wind,
though it was a punishment for those prior to me.

[His ﷺ Household ؓ]

[It is from among his ﷺ unique particulars that:]

» [it is mentioned] in an *athar* (tradition of the Companions ؓ) that his ﷺ family shall be upon the highest peak of Paradise

60. Holy Qur'ān, Sūrat ar-Ra'd (13), Verse 11.

» [it is mentioned] in a ḥadīth:

مَثَلُ أَهْلِ بَيْتِي مثلُ سَفِيْنَةِ نُوْحٍ ، مَنْ رَكِبَهَا نَجا، وَمَنْ تَخَلَّفَ عَنْهَا غرق

The similitude of my household is that of the Ark of [Prophet] Nūḥ ﷺ; he who mounts it shall be saved, and he who remains away from it shall drown[61]

» verily, one who attaches himself to them ﷺ and to the Qur'ān, does not go astray
» they ﷺ are a recourse for the Community amid differences
» they ﷺ are the leaders of the inhabitants of Paradise
» Allāh ﷻ has promised not to punish them ﷺ
» Allāh ﷻ shall cast into the Fire [of Hell] anyone who has any grudge against them ﷺ
» true faith shall not enter the heart of any one unless he loves them ﷺ for Allāh's ﷻ sake, and due to their proximity to him ﷺ
» one who fights against them ﷺ is as if he is fighting alongside the Dajjāl
» whoever extends to them a hand [of support], he ﷺ shall remunerate him on the Day of Judgement
» there is none among them except that he shall have the right of intercession on the Day of Judgement
» a person stands from his seat [out of honour] for his brother but the Banū Hāshim do not stand for anyone.

[His ﷺ Companions ﷺ]

Some commands were issued during his ﷺ era but thereafter they were abrogated – his ﷺ Companions ﷺ were able to act upon them but no one else could act upon them after them ﷺ. Among them [are the following]:
» invalidating Ḥajj for 'Umrah – according to the majority
» temporary marriage (*mut'ah*) with women – according to [the opinions of] most of the Community, and
» supererogatory Ḥajj – according to what 'Umar ﷺ, 'Uthmān ﷺ and Abū Dharr ﷺ have taken. Muslim reported from Abū Dharr ﷺ, who said:

61. Aḥmad; al-Ḥākim, *al-Mustadrak*; as-Suyūṭī, *ad-Durr al-Manthūr*, etc.

لَا تَصِحُّ الْمُتْعَتَانِ إِلَّا لَنَا خَاصَّةً

Two kinds of mut'ah (supererogatory and temporary) are not permitted, except specifically for us[62]

- divorce at the instance of the wife (*khul'*) – according to what Abū Bakr ibn 'Abdullāh al-Muzanī has taken
- reciting the Qur'ān with meaning
- incumbency of hosting guests
- spending wealth that is in excess [of one's needs]
- enslaving the debtor
- bathing not being obliged without spermatic ejaculation
- choosing between fasting in Ramaḍān and paying ransom (*fidyah*)
- prohibition to visit graves
- amassing more than three sacrificial animals
- centrifuging inside a vessel
- a fornicator marrying a chaste woman, and a fornicatress marrying a chaste man
- fighting [a battle] during the holy month[s]
- incumbency of bequest for parents and close relatives
- the widow's waiting for a period of one year [before she may remarry]
- the bearing of twenty [Believers] against two hundred [non-Believers]
- distribution of inheritance among those who are present
- minors and slaves to seek permission [to enter] during the three times [of the day]
- praying a major portion of the night
- inheriting through oath and migration
- accountability for the [intrapersonal] speaking of one's ego
- imprisonment for unlawful sexual intercourse
- discretionary punishment (*ta'zīr*) for destroying [another's] property
- testimony of a non-Muslim
- the Believers' praying seated behind an imām who is seated, even though without an excuse
- the Friday sermon after the ritual prayer
- *wuḍū'* for one who [uses something that] fire has touched
- disapproval of expressing delight during the sermon

62. Muslim, *al-Musnad aṣ-Ṣaḥīḥ*.

» prohibition of women adorning themselves with gold
» prohibition of begging for one who has food for a day and a night
» execution of [death penalty on] the alcoholic at the fourth occasion
» prohibition of burying the dead during the detested times.

The Mālikī [scholars] go with [the opinion] that the ḥadīth:

لَا يُجْلَدُ فَوْقَ عَشَرَةِ أَسْوَاطٍ إِلَّا فِيْ حَدٍّ

There is no whipping over ten stripes except for ḥadd (punishments)[63]

was specific to his ﷺ era because this amount was sufficient for the offender.

[Not Standing in Front of Him ﷺ in Ritual Prayer]

It is from among his ﷺ unique particulars – according to what al-Qāḍī 'Iyāḍ has narrated: "It is not permitted for anyone to lead him ﷺ in ritual prayer – because it is not correct to stand in front of him ﷺ in ritual prayer or otherwise, with or without an excuse, for Allāh ﷻ has proscribed the Believers from doing that."

[His ﷺ Having No Intercessor]

He ﷺ has no intercessor. He ﷺ said:

أَئِمَّتُكُمْ شُفَعَاؤُكُمْ

Your imāms are your intercessors[64]

and that is why Abū Bakr ؓ said:

مَا كَانَ لِابْنِ أَبِيْ قُحَافَةَ أَنْ يَتَقَدَّمَ بَيْنَ يَدَيْ
رَسُوْلِ اللهِ صَلَّى اللهُ عَلَيْهِ وَآلِهِ وَسَلَّمَ

The son of Abū Quḥāfah has no right to step ahead of the Messenger of Allāh ﷺ.

63. Al-Bukhārī, *al-Jāmi' aṣ-Ṣaḥīḥ*; Muslim, *al-Musnad aṣ-Ṣaḥīḥ*, etc.
64. Al-Qurṭubī: *al-Jāmi' li-Aḥkām al-Qur'ān*, etc.

[Honours of His ﷺ Companions ﷺ]

[It is from among his ﷺ unique particulars that] among his ﷺ Companions ﷺ, the partakers in [the Battle of] Badr are specified with having more than four *takbīrs* (*Allāhu Akbar*) pronounced at their funerals, as a distinction of their superiority.

[Furthermore,] it is among his ﷺ unique particulars that among his ﷺ Companions ﷺ is:

» one ﷺ upon whose death the Divine Throne convulsed in joy of meeting his ﷺ soul – seventy thousand angels, who had never set foot on earth prior to his ﷺ death, attended his ﷺ funeral[65]
» one whom ﷺ the angels bathed[66]
» one who resembles [Angel] Jibrīl ﷺ[67]
» [one who resembles Prophet] Ibrāhīm ﷺ
» [one who resembles Prophet] Nūḥ ﷺ
» [one who resembles Prophet] Mūsā ﷺ
» [one who resembles Prophet] ʿĪsā ﷺ
» [one who resembles Prophet] Yūsuf ﷺ
» [one who resembles Prophet] Luqmān the Wise ﷺ; and
» [one who resembles] the Holder of [the title] Yā-Sīn ﷺ.

[The Names 'al-Ḥasan' and 'al-Ḥusayn' ﷺ]

[It is from among his ﷺ unique particulars that it is mentioned] in *Ṭabaqāt ibn Saʿd* on the authority of ʿUmar ibn Sulaymān, who said: "Al-Ḥasan and al-Ḥusayn are two names from names of the inhabitants of Paradise. They were not [used] during the Era of Ignorance (*Jāhiliyyah*)."

[Naming Children After Prophets ﷺ]

[Furthermore,] therein [i.e. *Ṭabaqāt ibn Saʿd*] is [also a report] by Saʿīd ibn al-Musayyib ﷺ that it was disapproved to name one's children after the names of Prophets ﷺ.

---

65. It was Saʿd ibn Muʿādh ﷺ. (al-Bukhārī, *al-Jāmiʿ aṣ-Ṣaḥīḥ*; an-Nasāʾī, *as-Sunan*, etc.)
66. It was Ḥanzalah ﷺ. (at-Tirmidhī, *al-Jāmiʿ*, etc.)
67. It was Diḥyah al-Kalbī ﷺ. (an-Nasāʾī, *as-Sunan*)

[Greeting Him ﷺ in His ﷺ Grave]

[It is mentioned] in *Jāmi' ath-Thawrī* and *Muṣannaf 'Abdurrazzāq*, on the authority of Sa'īd ibn al-Musayyib ﵁ that he saw some people greeting him ﷺ with peace. He said: "No prophet ﵇ remains in his ﵇ grave longer than forty days before he ﵇ is raised up."[68]

[His ﷺ Certainty]

Imām al-Ḥaramayn, in *an-Nihāyah*, and ar-Rāfi'ī in *ash-Sharḥ aṣ-Ṣaghīr*, have mentioned a ḥadīth:

أَنَا أَكْرَمُ عَلَى رَبِّيْ مِنْ أَن يَتْرُكَنِيْ فِيْ قَبْرِيْ بَعْدَ ثَلَاثٍ

My honour with my Lord ﷻ is greater than Him ﷻ leaving me in my grave for more than three days.

[It is mentioned] in *Kifāyat al-Mu'taqid* of al-Yāfi'ī: "Some [scholars] said: 'Certainty is: i. a name, ii. a custom, iii. a science, iv. an object, and v. a verity.

i. The name and
ii. the custom are for the general public
iii. the science is the science of certainty – for the Friends [of Allāh ﷻ]
iv. the object of certainty is for specific Friends [of Allāh ﷻ] and
v. the verity of certainty is for the Prophets ﵈, whereas

the reality of the verity of the certainty is what our Prophet [Muḥammad] ﷺ is specified with.'"

Shaykh Tājuddīn ibn 'Aṭā'ullāh said: "The Prophets ﵈ are aware of the realities of the affairs, and the Friends [of Allāh ﷻ] are aware of their representation." This is also a saying of al-Yāfi'ī.

Shaykh 'Abdulqādir al-Jīlānī has differentiated between what the Prophets ﵈ hear and what the Friends [of Allāh ﷻ] hear; the Revelation given to Prophets ﵈ is called *Kalām*, whereas the Revelation given to the Friends [of Allāh ﷻ] is called *Ḥadīth*. As for the *Kalām*, it is binding to accept it; whoever denies it is a disbeliever, whereas one who denies the *Ḥadīth* [of the Friends of Allāh ﷻ] does not become a disbeliever.

68. The Prophet Muḥammad ﷺ responds to the greeting of peace made to him ﷺ, as is mentioned in many ḥadīths, such as that related by Abū Hurayrah ﵁: "The Prophet ﷺ said: 'If any one of you greets me, Allāh ﷻ returns my soul to me and I respond to the greeting." (Abū Dāwūd, *as-Sunan*).

Abū 'Umar ad-Dimishqī aṣ-Ṣūfī said: "Allāh 🕮 has obligated presentation of miracles upon the Prophets 🕮 – so that the people may believe in them; He 🕮 has obligated concealing miracles upon the Friends [of Allāh 🕮] so that they are not taken to task."

Abu'l-'Abbās al-Marwazī as-Sayyārī said: "Risk is for the Prophets 🕮, whispering is for the Friends [of Allāh 🕮], and contemplation is for the general public."

In *Baḥr al-Kalām*, an-Nasafī said: "The souls of the Prophets 🕮 leave their bodies and take the forms of musk and camphor. The souls of martyrs leave their bodies and reside in the hearts of green birds."

[Honours for Prophets 🕮]

It is among the unique particulars of the Prophets 🕮:

» verily, there shall be thrones of gold erected for them at the Station [in the Plain of the Great Gathering on the Day of Judgement] upon which they shall sit. This shall not be the case for any one but them 🕮.

Sa'īd ibn al-Musayyib 🕮 said: "There is no religious seclusion (*i'tikāf*) other than in the Masjid of the Prophet 🕮." An-Nasā'ī has taken this from the ḥadīth of Qutaybah.

[It is mentioned] in the *Karāmāt al-Awliyā'* of Khāl ibn as-Sunnī, on the authority of Bishr ibn al-Ḥārith, that these ḥadīths were mentioned in his presence on the answering of supplications, etc., and so he said: "I do not refute any of these but two things: [use of] gold and walking on water; because none have been given them other than the Prophets 🕮."

An-Nawawī mentions a ḥadīth:

مَا مِنْ مَوْلُودٍ يُولَدُ إِلَّا نَخَسَهُ الشَّيْطَانُ . . . ، إِلَّا مَرْيَمَ وَابْنَهَا

No baby is born except that Shaytan nips it ...,
except for Maryam 🕮 and her son 🕮.[69]

The apparent side of this ḥadīth specifies this merit to Prophet 'Īsā 🕮 and his mother 🕮, whereas al-Qāḍī 'Iyāḍ has hinted that all the Prophets 🕮 share this [merit].

---

69. Muslim, *al-Musnad aṣ-Ṣaḥīḥ*, *Kitāb al-Faḍā'il*, *Bāb Faḍā'il 'Īsā* 🕮, Ḥadīth 6133.

[It is mentioned] in *Ḥāshiyat al-Kashshāf* of aṭ-Ṭībī in reference to the saying of Allāh ﷻ:

ٱلْـَٔـٰنَ خَفَّفَ ٱللَّهُ عَنكُمْ

Now, Allāh ﷻ has lightened (the burden) from you (O Prophet Muḥammad ﷺ)...[70]

that as-Sulamī reported from an-Naṣrābādī: "This lightening [of the burden] was for the Community rather than for the Messenger ﷺ. How can one ﷺ seek to have lightened in order to gain the opposite when the burden of the trust of prophethood [already] weighs him ﷺ down? And how can he ﷺ seek [it], when it is he ﷺ who says: 'It is with You ﷻ that I leap' and 'It is with You ﷻ that I go about'? When it is such with a person, how can it be lightened from him ﷺ, and how can it be burdensome upon him ﷺ?"

[It is mentioned] in *Ta'rīkh ibn 'Asākir*, on the authority of Ḥātim ar-Rāzī, who said: "Since when Allāh ﷻ created Prophet Ādam ﷺ, there has been no Community that has been preserving the traces of their Prophet ﷺ, except for this Community." Then, a man said to him: "O Abū Ḥātim, they sometimes report a ḥadīth that has no basis." He replied: "Their scholars can distinguish between the sound and the fabricated. Thus, their reporting an incorrect ḥadīth is to make it clear to those who come after them that they have distinguished the traces and preserved them."

As-Subkī said: "Verily, one who prays with the Prophet ﷺ, and then deliberately stands up with him ﷺ for the fifth [unit], or he deliberately makes the salutation after two [units with him ﷺ], his prayer is not void."

That is because it is possible for the Revelation to have come to him ﷺ with regards to addition or subtraction. As for after him ﷺ, whenever the worshipper being led by the imām follows him in that [as aforementioned], his prayer stands void.

[His ﷺ Unique Qualities]

In *Sharḥ as-Sunan*, Ibn al-'Arabī mentioned, among his ﷺ unique particulars:

» travelling alone due to his ﷺ being safe from Shayṭān, as opposed to anyone else.

70. Holy Qur'ān, Sūrat al-Anfāl (8), Verse 66.

In *at-Tanwīr*, Ibn Diḥyah said: "Allāh ﷻ specified His ﷻ Prophet ﷺ with a thousand qualities. Among them are:

» Allāh ﷻ and His ﷻ angels invoking blessings on him ﷺ

and among them are:

» beholding the Beatific Vision
» proximity and closeness [with Allāh ﷻ]
» intercession
» intermediation
» superior merit
» lofty station
» the Burāq
» the Heavenly Ascent (*Mi'rāj*)
» offering ritual prayer whilst leading the Prophets عليهم السلام
» being taken on the Night Journey (*Isrā'*)
» being given pleasure
» allowed to seek [from Allāh ﷻ]
» the [Fount of] al-Kawthar
» listening to the saying [of Allāh ﷻ]
» completion of the favour [of Allāh ﷻ]
» forgiveness of the past and the future
» expansion of the chest
» removal of the burden
» elevation of [his ﷺ] tribute
» might of victory
» descension of tranquility
» being given the Book; the Seven Oft-Repeated Verses (*as-Sab' al-Mathānī*); the Tremendous Qur'ān

that he ﷺ was sent as:

» a mercy to the worlds
» adjudicator among the people according to what Allāh ﷻ has shown him ﷺ – this is not for anyone else among the Prophets عليهم السلام – upon him and upon them be blessings and peace
» the Tremendous Qur'ān speaks to him ﷺ at will
» swearing by his ﷺ name
» answering his ﷺ prayers
» witnessing among the Prophets عليهم السلام and the [Prophetic] Communities on the Day of Judgement

» love [of Allāh ﷻ]
» intimacy [with Allāh ﷻ]
» and other such multitude of qualities that are not encompassable."
Ends [Ibn Diḥyah's statement].

[Preferring Him ﷺ Over One's Own Self]

I studied the book *Ḥusn al-Iqtiṣāṣ li-mā Yata'allaqu bi'l-Ikhtiṣāṣ* of Shaykh Badruddīn ibn ad-Damāmīnī, and I saw in it that he said: "It is among his ﷺ unique particulars: the obligation to protect him ﷺ with [one's own] life."

Ibn al-Munayyir[71] said: "Allāh ﷻ has obligated for his ﷺ sake that he ﷺ be preferred over [one's own] life, and that he ﷺ be more beloved to every Believer than their own selves."

Thus, on the day of [the Battle of] Uḥud, Sa'd ؓ said: "It shall by my throat before yours ﷺ." This is among his ﷺ unique particulars, and it is undisputed that this is not incumbent on anyone other than for him ﷺ. Is it permitted to do likewise for the sake of someone else? Apparently, it is not permitted, based on the analogy of the impermissibility of sacrificing water [to another] for purification purposes, and for drinking purposes if it contributes to the death of the one who possesses the water.

[His ﷺ Descendants are Not Slaves]

He said: "Just observe, is there a prohibition for him ﷺ to marry a bondmaid? Their reasoning is that whoever marries a bondmaid, his child from her will be a slave, whereas his ﷺ status is above anything of the sort. Therein is the indication that the al-Ḥasanī and al-Ḥusaynī nobles (*sharīf*) are prohibited from marrying bondmaids – that it will lead to their children from them being enslaved, whereas the status of the Master of the Creation ﷺ is too lofty for any of his ﷺ descendants to be enslaved."

And when Ibn al-Munayyir spoke regarding the ḥadīth in the *Commentary on al-Bukhārī*, mentioned in the chapter *Man Malaka mina'l-'Arabi Raqīqan – Whoever Acquired the Ownership of a Slave*, wherein is the saying:

71. He is Nāṣiruddīn ibn al-Munayyir (d. 683AH /1284AH).

أَعْتِقْهَا، فَإِنَّهَا مِنْ وَلَدِ إِسْمَاعِيلَ

Free it, for it is from among the children of Ismā'īl ﷺ[72]

he said: "With me, it necessitates there being a distinction in the Arabs being owned [as slaves]; [especially] the specification of the nobles (*sharīf*) among the descendants of Fāṭimah ﷺ. Thus, if we were to hypothesise that an al-Ḥasanī or an al-Ḥusaynī was to marry a bondmaid, it would render it impossible for us to oppose that the child from her would not be enslaved.

Its proof is the saying of the Prophet ﷺ:

أَعْتِقْهَا، فَإِنَّهَا مِنْ وَلَدِ إِسْمَاعِيلَ

Free it, for it is from among the children of Ismā'īl ﷺ.[73]

Its being from the descendants of Prophet Isma'īl ﷺ entails it being recommended [to free it], and therefore what we have mentioned is tantamount to absolute unlawfulness [in enslaving the descendants of Prophet Muḥammad ﷺ]. Opposing this [opinion] is extremely difficult."

[Fragrance of the Prophet ﷺ]

He [i.e. Ibn al-Munayyir] said: "It is among his ﷺ unique particulars: that whenever he ﷺ would take a path that someone else might follow, the latter would recognise that he ﷺ took [this path] by his ﷺ fragrance. Al-Bukhārī mentioned this, on the authority of Jābir ﷺ, in his *at-Ta'rīkh al-Kabīr.*

Isḥāq ibn Rāhiwayh said: 'His ﷺ fragrance emitted without applying perfume.'

Some [of the scholars] have enumerated this among his ﷺ unique particulars."

Ends [Ibn al-Munayyir's statement].

[His ﷺ Telling Stories of the Past and Future]

It is among that which is [mentioned] in the *Tadhkirah* of Shaykh Badruddīn ibn aṣ-Ṣāḥib: "It was the desire of the Prophets ﷺ that inclined towards finding a man who would tell them stories of the previous peoples and the future peoples.

72. Al-Bukhārī, *al-Jāmi' aṣ-Ṣaḥīḥ*; Muslim, *al-Musnad aṣ-Ṣaḥīḥ*.
73. Al-Bukhārī, *al-Jāmi' aṣ-Ṣaḥīḥ*; Muslim, *al-Musnad aṣ-Ṣaḥīḥ*.

Thus came the Prophet [Muḥammad ﷺ] [as a fulfilment] to all of those desires, and he ﷺ told many stories, and he ﷺ filled the world with goodness."

[The Black Spot – Removed]

In *at-Tawshīḥ*, Ibn as-Subkī said: "I heard [my] father saying: 'It was asked about the black spot that was removed from the heart of the Prophet ﷺ when his ﷺ chest was split open in his ﷺ childhood, and the angel's saying: 'It is Shayṭān's [influential] portion in you ﷺ,' that was the black spot that Allāh ﷻ had created in the hearts of humans, receiving everything that Shayṭān casts into it. It was removed from the heart of the Prophet ﷺ, and thus, no space remained inside it that would receive what Shayṭān could cast into it.' He said: 'This is the meaning of the ḥadīth: *Shayṭān never had a portion (of influence) in it.* As for what the angel had cleaned out, it was from the human innate disposition, and thus the acceptor [of Shayṭānic influence] was removed – that with which any wrongful accusation would not have been entertained [regardless].'

I asked him: 'Then why did Allāh ﷻ create this acceptor [of Shayṭānic deceptions] inside that Noble Person ﷺ when it was possible for Allāh ﷻ not to have created it therein.'

He replied: 'It is from among the absolute parts of the human. Its creation is the completion of the human form – which is necessary. He ﷻ removed it out of His ﷻ divine favour that became apparent later on.'

[My] brother saw [my] father after his death – there were many lights upon him, and he [i.e. my brother] knew in his heart that it was due to this discussion."

[His ﷺ Blessed Body is Fresh]

In *aṭ-Ṭabaqāt*, as-Subkī said: "It is not established with me that the body of any Friend [of Allāh ﷻ] be revived after many ages [have passed] and [after] it had become decomposed bones – after which it may live when it has been revived after a long time. This account has not reached us, and I do not believe that this has occurred with any of the Friends [of Allāh ﷻ]. [However,] there is no doubt in something like this happening for the Prophets عليهم السلام – something like this happening would be a [Prophetic] miracle, which [saintly] miracles cannot reach."

[ENDS]

Concluding Salutations by the Translator

O Allāh ﷻ, accept our humble efforts in recognising and celebrating the lofty and unique qualities and merits of Your Beloved Messenger Muḥammad ﷺ, without whom ﷺ we would have been lost in the darkness of this world; without whom ﷺ we would have been clasped in the evil grip of Shayṭān; without ﷺ whom we would have remained lower than beasts; without whom ﷺ we would have remained careless, carefree and oblivious of our very own existence.

We invoke Your ﷻ divine blessings, mercy and salutations upon him ﷺ for ever and ever, in a manner and quantity that You ﷻ wish to shower Your ﷻ divine blessings, mercy and salutations upon him ﷺ.
Āmīn, yā Rabb al-'Ālamīn, bi-jāhi Ṭā-Hā wa Yā-Sīn.

Ṭāhir Maḥmood Kiānī

Bibliography

Qur'ān

Abū Dāwūd, Sulaymān ibn al-Ash'ath ibn Isḥāq al-Azdī (202AH/817CE – 275AH/889CE). *as-Sunan*. Riyādh. Dārussalām. 3rd Edition. 1421AH/2000CE.

Al-Bukhārī, Abū 'Abdullāh Muḥammad ibn Ismā'īl ibn Ibrāhīm ibn al-Mughīrah ibn Bardizbah (194AH/809CE – 256AH/869CE). *al-Jāmi' aṣ-Ṣaḥīḥ*. Riyādh. Dārussalām. 3rd Edition. 1421AH/2000CE.

An-Nasā'ī, Abū 'Abdurraḥmān Aḥmad ibn Shu'ayb ibn 'Alī ibn Sinān (215AH/829CE – 303AH/915CE). *as-Sunan aṣ-Ṣughrā*. Riyādh. Dārussalām. 3rd Edition. 1421AH/2000CE.

As-Suyūṭī, Abu'l-Faḍl 'Abdurraḥmān ibn Abū Bakr Jalāluddīn (849AH/1445CE – 911AH/1505CE). *al-Khaṣā'iṣ aṣ-Ṣughrā* (Urdu). Translated by 'Allāmah 'Abdurrasūl Arshad. Lahore. Zia-ul-Qur'an Publications. Rabī' al-Awwal 1406ah.

As-Suyūṭī, Abu'l-Faḍl 'Abdurraḥmān ibn Abū Bakr Jalāluddīn (849AH/1445CE – 911AH/1505CE). "http://ansaralmostafa.mam9.com/t249-topic." *Ansar al-Mostafa*. October 10. Accessed October 10, 2015. http://ansaralmostafa.mam9.com/t249-topic.

At-Tibrīzī, Abū 'Abdullāh Muḥammad ibn 'Abdullāh al-Khaṭīb (D.741AH/1340CE). *Mishkāt al-Maṣābīḥ*. Beirut. Dar al-Kotob al-Ilmiyah. 1421AH/2003CE.

At-Tirmidhī, Abū 'Īsā Muḥammad ibn 'Īsā ibn Sawrah ibn Mūsāas-Sulamī (200AH/824CE – 279AH/892CE). *al-Jāmi' al-Mukhtaṣar*. Riyādh. Dārussalām. 3rd Edition. 1421AH/2000CE.

Ibn Mājah, Abū 'Abdullāh Muḥammad ibn Yazīd (209AH/824CE – 273AH/887CE). *as-Sunan*. Riyādh. Dārussalām. 3rd Edition. 1421AH/2000CE.

Lane, Edward William (1801 – 1876CE). *Arabic-English Lexicon (online version)*. London. Williams and Norgate. 1863CE.

Muslim, Abu'l-Ḥusayn Muslim ibn al-Ḥajjāj ibn Muslim al-Qushayrī an-Naysābūrī (206AH/821CE – 261AH/875CE). *al-Musnad aṣ-Ṣaḥīḥ*. Riyādh. Dārussalām. 3rd Edition. 1421AH/2000CE.

Waliyyullāh, Shāh Quṭbuddīn Aḥmad ibn Ibrāhīm ad-Dihlawī (1114AH/1703CE – 1176AH/1762CE). *Al-Fawz al-Kabīr fī Uṣūl at-Tafsīr – The Great Victory on Qur'ānic Hermeneutics*. Translated by Ṭāhir Maḥmood Kiānī. London. Ta-Ha Publishers Ltd. January 2014CE.

About the Translator

Ṭāhir Maḥmood Kiānī, son of the saintly Ḥājī Muḥammad Tāj 'Alī Kiānī (1356AH/1938CE – 1415AH/1995CE), is a graduate in Law and Islāmic Law. He teaches classical Arabic grammar and Islāmic sciences, writes and lectures on various topics, as well as translating from Urdu and classical Arabic into English. His most notable translations are *Mukhtaṣār al-Qudūrī – A manual of Islāmic Law According to the Ḥanafī School*, *Al-Fawz al-Kabīr – The Great Victory on Qur'ānic Hermeneutics*, *Qaṣīdat Aṭyab an-Nagham fī Madḥ Sayyid al-'Arab wa'l-'Ajam* ﷺ *– The Sweetest Melody* and *Ādāb aṣ-Ṣuḥbah - Etiquettes of Companionship (Imām ash-Sha'rānī)*.